# EVANGELISTIC PREACHING

*By*
*LLOYD M. PERRY*
*and*
*JOHN R. STRUBHAR*

MOODY PRESS
CHICAGO

© 1979 by
THE MOODY BIBLE INSTITUTE
OF CHICAGO

The use of selected references from various versions of the
Bible in this publication does not necessarily imply publisher
endorsement of the versions in their entirety.

**Library of Congress Cataloging in Publication Data**

Perry, Lloyd Merle.
  Evangelistic preaching.
  Bibliography: p. 199.
  1. Preaching. 2. Evangelistic work. I. Strubhar, John R.,
joint author. II. Title.

BV4211.2.P437     253     79-13312

ISBN 0-8024-2391-4

*Printed in the United States of America*

253
P46

# Contents

60347

# *Foreword*

PULPIT EVANGELISM is not a luxury; it is a necessity. Sad to say, in some churches it is a travesty. Because of that, I am happy for this book. This book calls us to a *true* pulpit evangelism. It calls us back to biblical truths that must not be replaced with pragmatic methods that "get results." It reminds us that God is seeking fruit, not "results," and that fruit can come only from life.

It also calls us back to the historical roots of evangelism in the church. I know of no other book on evangelistic preaching that builds on such a solid foundation from church history. Too many books on evangelism have majored on the few well-known preachers of modern days. This book reminds us that there were great evangelistic preachers in other ages, preachers who can teach us a great deal about winning the lost.

The authors are courageous. They dare to point out the difference between true evangelistic preaching and "Christian salesmanship" that turns out to be only religious propagandizing or the pressure of a great personality. They avoid simplistic approaches that confuse methods with principles and bypass the character of the preacher. If anything, they dare to show us that true, biblical evangelistic preaching is costly and difficult. There is more to it than the preaching of a message; there is also the building of the messenger, the preparation of the message, and the examination of motives.

It is my hope and prayer that this book will call preachers and churches back to the theological and historical roots of evangelism. I am sure that the rediscovery of the roots will hasten the production of the fruits.

WARREN W. WIERSBE

6

# Introduction

THE CHURCH needs evangelism to save herself from the sterility of a merely cultural religion. The life of the church and her hope for the future lie in her reproductive power, which is evangelism. The local congregation must evangelize or die.

Some churches seem to belong to the cult of the comfortable. They seem to have become satisfied with themselves. They are neglecting their outreach responsibilities and are thus missing great privileges. Churches grow and are especially blessed when high priority is given to effective evangelism.

The word is out among some pastors, church leaders, seminary professors, and ministerial students that evangelistic preaching does not work anymore. Some suggest that in our different world of today, only inner-city reclamation, discussion groups, world-awareness studies, renewal of liturgy, and other kinds of "modern" ministry can be used to call people to God. It is the conviction of the authors of this book, however, that biblical evangelistic preaching can still be a very effective means of reaching souls for the Savior.

The time has come for a revival atmosphere to be created by the Holy Spirit in the churches of our land. When individuals get "on fire for God," the unsaved will be prompted to come and see them "burn." The health curve of the church across the centuries can be traced in accordance with the evangelistic fervor in the pulpits. The church must have the same burden as her Lord, of whom it was declared, "[He came] to seek and to save that which was lost" (Luke 19:10).

A preacher who has an average of two hundred eighty listeners a week will have some six thousand hours of time entrusted to him in a year. Anyone who claims all those hours of human life for listening to his preaching has a very great challenge. Integrity requires that he either learn how to preach or else quit. Someone has figured out that there are about five million sermons preached each year in this country. Preachers must not place those sermons on the altar and expect God to send His fire upon them unless they are adequate and have cost the preacher his best effort.

The time has come for the church to major not only in personal evangelism, but for the church and especially the preacher to major in pulpit evangelism.

This book is an attempt to survey the emphases and possible trends in American evangelistic preaching through a study of selected trade books and textbooks in the field of evangelistic and homiletic theory.

The book is limited in several respects. In the first place, so far as is possible, personalities are not highlighted. The preponderance of literature on the lives of famous evangelists and their noteworthy sermons is completely bypassed in favor of homiletic principles and sermonic technique. Likewise, the works dealing with the theology of evangelism are not explored.

This work seeks to establish objective criteria for engaging in pulpit evangelism. That is, the methodological and structural aspects of evangelistic sermonic theory are analyzed to secure an objective base and structural method for evangelistic preaching. To do this, we have chosen to employ four of five canons of classical rhetoric as a scheme to collect and organize material in a logical manner. Basically, classical rhetoric is a study of the theory of speechmaking. According to Aristotle in *The Rhetoric*, "Rhetoric may be defined as the faculty of

8

discovering all the possible means of persuasion in any subject."[1] In the works of Aristotle, Cicero, and Quintilian, classical rhetoric reached its zenith. The five canons are:

1. Invention (*inventio*) : The origination, or discovery, of ideas, or concepts, of a speech.
2. Arrangement (*dispositio*): The organization of material discovered into logical or topical progression, with some consideration of the "weight" of material.
3. Style (*elocutio*) : The process of phrasing in language the ideas invented and arranged.
4. Memory (*memoria*) : The retention of ideas or thoughts in such a way that they can be reproduced. (This is omitted in this work.)
5. Delivery (*pronunciatio*) : The presentation of ideas that have been invented, arranged, phrased, and memorized; it is concerned with both the audible code of speech and the visible code of speech.

An analysis of evangelistic preaching is sorely needed, because very little has been written on the subject. We were able to find only five books bearing the title "evangelistic preaching."[2]

One possible reason for the scarcity of material on the subject is that some schools of thought have divided homiletics and evangelistic preaching, placing the latter in "halieutics," a division of practical theology dealing with missions. It is our contention and that of Edmund Clowney in *Preaching and Biblical Theology* (1961) that this division has been unfortunate and may, in part, explain why evangelistic preaching has

1. Lester Thonssen, ed., *Selected Readings in Rhetoric and Public Speaking*, p. 36.
2. Ozora S. Davis, *Evangelistic Preaching;* D. P. Thomson, ed., *The Modern Evangelistic Address;* Roy H. Short, *Evangelistic Preaching;* Faris D. Whitesell, *Evangelistic Preaching and the Old Testament;* and V. L. Stanfield, *Effective Evangelistic Preaching.*

been isolated so often from objective homiletic sermonic principles.[3]

One must understand what evangelism is before he can fully comprehend the definitive elements of evangelistic preaching. Dr. Robert E. Speer, late secretary emeritus of the Board of Foreign Missions of the Presbyterian Church in the United States, said, "Evangelism is the presentation of the truth and life of Christianity both by word and by deed, with a view to persuading men to accept it, and to believe in Jesus Christ as Lord and Saviour and in God through Him and to give their lives to His service."[4] J. I. Packer noted the famous definition of evangelism formulated by the Archbishops' Committee in their report in 1918: "To evangelize is so to present Christ Jesus in the power of the Holy Spirit, that men shall come to put their trust in God through Him, to accept Him as their Saviour, and serve Him as their King in the fellowship of His Church."[5] According to the late Paul Little, formerly an associate professor of evangelism at Trinity Divinity School, probably the greatest definition of evangelism is the one formulated by the Student Volunteer Missionary Union: "The presentation of the Gospel in such a manner to every soul in this world that the responsibility for what is done with it shall no longer rest upon the Christian church or any individual Christian, but shall rest upon each man's head for himself."[6] From these three comprehensive definitions, one may conclude that evangelism is the effective presentation of the gospel in such a manner that the hearer understands its implications and is brought to the place of decision for Christ.

3. Particularly is this true of Tjeerd Hoekstra, *Gereformeerde Homiletiek* pp. 31, 185; Karl Djik, *De Dienst der Prediking* p. 96; and Abraham Kuyper, *Encyclopaedia der Heilege Godgeleerheid*, 3:488: "The kerygma with which the church comes of the unbelievers, is so wholly something other than the homily in the midst of the believers, that it would be illogical to wish to join the technical theory for both under one concept."
4. John R. Mott, ed., *Evangelism for the World Today*, p. 103.
5. J. I. Packer, *Evangelism and the Sovereignty of God*, pp. 37-38.
6. A. J. Broomhall, *Time for Action*, p. 43.

In the history of homiletics, evangelistic preaching has been described in various terms. Originally, *revivalistic* preaching was the term in vogue. Early works dealing with evangelistic preaching, such as Kern's *The Ministry of the Congregation* (1897), Broadus's *On the Preparation and Delivery of Sermons* (revised 1898), and Etter's *The Preacher and His Sermon* (1891), employed this terminology. According to Etter, who wrote nineteen pages on the subject, "revivalistic" preaching has a twofold emphasis, namely, to convert the sinner and to revive the saints.[7]

Later, the term *soul-winning* preaching became the label for evangelistic preaching. Frederick E. Taylor devoted thirty pages to soul-winning preaching in his book *The Evangelistic Church* (1927). He suggested that if such preaching is to be effective, it must be prayerful, positive, practical, personal, and persuasive.[8] Dr. Andrew Blackwood, the famed homilist and pastoral theologian at Princeton Theological Seminary, characterized soul-winning preaching as biblical in substance, doctrinal in form, and popular in style. More specifically, he said, "The sermon that saves the soul brings the hearer face to face with the Son of God and moves him to accept Jesus as Saviour and Lord. In every soul-winning message there is a note of urgency, 'Now is the accepted time.' "[9]

Frederick E. Taylor was a contemporary of Ozora S. Davis, who wrote a book entitled *Evangelistic Preaching* (1921). In that work, Davis defined evangelistic sermons as "those sermons which were designed primarily to publish the gospel as a message to those who never had heard it or who needed to hear some new aspects of it presented."[10] And Dr. Blackwood, who also used the term "soul-winning," was a contemporary of Dr. Faris D. Whitesell. In 1947 Whitesell wrote a book titled *Evangelistic Preaching and the Old Testament*. In that work

7. John W. Etter, *The Preacher and His Sermon*, p. 236.
8. Frederick E. Taylor, *The Evangelistic Church*, pp. 125-52.
9. Andrew W. Blackwood, *Evangelism in the Home Church*, p. 70.
10. Davis, p. 61.

11

Whitesell definitively described evangelistic preaching as "preaching at its best." "It is," said Whitesell:

> preaching adapted to the highest ends of the gospel—turning men from sin and darkness to salvation and light. Evangelistic preaching is preaching with a mission—an immediate and all-important mission—winning a verdict in favor of the Lord Jesus Christ. The evangelistic sermon is an all-out effort to bring the lost to Christ. A devotional or inspirational sermon, with an evangelistic kite-tail attached, is not an evangelistic sermon. A sermon with a mild evangelistic strain or color running through it, is not an evangelistic sermon. These sermons may be good and perfectly appropriate for many occasions, but such preaching ought not to be called evangelistic preaching. The true evangelistic sermon is a *planned, organized and concentrated drive toward the goal of decisions for Christ* (italics ours) .[11]

This emphasis on a drive toward a decision has become a hallmark of evangelistic preaching and has expressed itself even in the new terminology employed for evangelistic preaching— *kerygmatic preaching.*

In 1965, *Effective Evangelistic Preaching,* by Dr. Vernon L. Stanfield, professor of preaching at New Orleans Baptist Theological Seminary, was published. In that small volume, Stanfield discussed the basic presuppositions, central message, occasions, goals, and qualities of evangelistic preaching, and also the construction and delivery of an evangelistic sermon. He analyzed the invitation used in an evangelistic message and included six evangelistic sermons. He defined evangelistic preaching as "the proclamation of the good news concerning the redemptive acts of God in Christ, by one who experientially knows Jesus Christ, in order to lead others to receive Christ as their Saviour and their Lord."[12] J. Winston Pearce also used the term *evangelistic* in his work *Planning Your Preaching* (1967) .[13]

11. Whitesell, p. 28.
12. Stanfield, p. 11.
13. J. Winston Pearce, *Planning Your Preaching,* pp. 118-37.

12

H. C. Brown, Jr., in his book *A Quest for Reformation in Preaching*, employed the term "kerygmatic" to describe evangelistic preaching. He defined the evangelistic objective by explaining "Men are saved by hearing the gospel preached or explained and by committing themselves to Jesus Christ."[14] In 1972, Dr. J. Daniel Baumann formerly the department chairman of pastoral ministries and director of field education at Bethel Theological Seminary, wrote a book entitled *An Introduction to Contemporary Preaching*. Said Dr. Baumann, "Kerygmatic preaching is also called proclamation or evangelistic preaching. . . . Proclamation is unashamed evangelistic preaching that calls man to make a personal decision regarding Jesus Christ as Saviour and Lord."[15]

It is our opinion that all these designations—revivalistic,[16] soul-winning, evangelistic, and kerygmatic—refer essentially to the same thing, namely, the proclamation of the gospel of Christ in such a way that men will repent of their sin by turning to Christ, embracing Him as Savior and Lord.

This particular investigation into evangelistic preaching is limited to the contributions of those men who were born in the United States and whose works were printed by American publishing houses. Moreover, the authors of the works are all Protestants.

"The dominant image of evangelizing today," said Dr. Seward Hiltner, professor of theology and personality at

14. H. C. Brown, Jr., *A Quest for Reformation in Preaching*, pp. 141-42.
15. J. Daniel Baumann, *An Introduction to Contemporary Preaching*, p. 207.
16. Although it may be argued that revivalistic preaching is not the same as evangelistic preaching, the advice of George Sweazey is worth noting: "Strictly speaking, a revival is not evangelism. Only a Christian life which has already been started can be revived. But in practice, revival and evangelism are often combined. The same appeal which brings the unchurched to dedication can bring church members to rededication. A service which is radiant with the sense of the Divine presence can introduce the unsaved to Christ while it is keeping Him as a daily reality in the lives of the saved" (George E. Sweazey, *Effective Evangelism: The Greatest Work in the World*, p. 161). Etter observed: "A true revival of religion is a movement among the people, produced by the agency of God's people and the working of God's Spirit, resulting in the quickening of his children and the conversion of sinners" (Etter, pp. 238-39).

Princeton Theological Seminary, "is the huge hall or arena, an impassioned preacher sharply spotlighted, with arms so held that they entreat the hearers to decide for Jesus Christ and then come down the aisles."[17] Such an image results from equating evangelistic preaching with personalities rather than principles. True, well-meaning evangelists in the past have sometimes resorted to less than honorable techniques in getting their message across. It is true that they have concentrated more on the method than on the message and that professionalism has often detracted from genuine evangelistic endeavor. As Ernest Thompson wrote of evangelist B. Fay Mills, "His careful preparation, thorough organization and high pressure methods gave it business efficiency and promoted mass conversions, which sometimes resembled mass production."[18] But such actions in the past do not negate the validity of evangelistic preaching today or the need to discover homiletic principles that will enable the preacher to do the work of the evangelist more effectively. J. Winston Pearce listed nine reasons why evangelistic preaching is still a viable option and sorely needed in our generation:

> The whole approach of evangelism is foreign to today's thought and spirit. . . .
>
> The world does not care what the churches are talking about when the evangelistic message is proclaimed. . . .
>
> There is a strong tendency in certain areas to remove God and Christ, law and gospel from the center of all ethical and moral thinking. . . .
>
> There is great confusion being caused by the social existentialists. . . .
>
> There is an alarming disregard for individual responsibility. . . .
>
> The current fad of "religionless Christianity" is gaining momentum, that is, the disregard for the church in all of its traditional expressions. . . .

17. Seward Hiltner, *Ferment in the Ministry*, p. 112.
18. Ernest T. Thompson, *Changing Emphases in American Preaching*, p. 103.

14

> The modern pastor has made appeals solely to the "Christian element" in the congregation. He has not delivered the whole counsel of God. . . .
>
> The modern pastor has become frightened by numbers which are evangelistic hallmarks. (He must remember that numbers represent people for whom Christ died.) . . .
>
> The decaying morality in America is running unchecked.[19]

This book is written from the traditional rhetorical perspective, in which the emphasis is on the source, that is, the speaker—his character (ethos) and speaking skills. However, during the last ten or fifteen years, due to extensive research in the field of communication theory, the pendulum has swung from an emphasis on the source to an emphasis on the receptor, or audience.

According to C. David Mortensen of the University of Wisconsin,

> The concept of communication theory should be taken as an umbrella term for a host of general principles and orienting statements designed to specify causes and key relationships among given facets of communicative behavior. Underlying his vast range of theoretical ideas is a diverse assortment of concepts, insights, and research findings. Some discoveries emerge from investigations on the psychological factors involved in the creation and interpretation of messages. Others focus on the social influences in communication, particularly the roles and cross-currents of tension and conflict in face-to-face settings. Still others relate to the impact of the physical environment and the larger role of culture in communication.[20]

Effective communication requires at least three elements, "the source, the message, and destination (receptor)."[21] Furthermore, communication takes place when the worlds of

19. Pearce, pp. 119-28.
20. C. David Mortensen, ed., *Basic Readings in Communication Theory*, p. 1.
21. Wilbur Schramm, "How Communication Works," in Mortenson, p. 28.

experience, evaluations, and symbols (words) are properly related from both the speaker's and the listener's point of view. Dr. Raymond W. McLaughlin, department head of homiletics and speech at Conservative Baptist Seminary, stated: "From the speaker's point of view the communicative act involves seeing life's experiences, evaluating them, and describing them. From the hearer's point of view the communicative act occurs when he receives messages and understands them with relative accuracy."[22]

The growing trend toward audience awareness in speaking is further explained by Ralph L. Lewis, professor of speech at Asbury Theological Seminary:

> It takes two to make a speech—a speaker and a listener. Thus human wants, needs, desires, and wishes are the basis for persuasive speaking. The very life and breath of successful speaking is to be audience-centered. The speaker must begin where the hearers are; he must engage their vital interests, relate to their basic needs and try to lift them to the level of willing, responsive listeners.[23]

From a rhetorical viewpoint, there is a great scarcity of works relating to evangelistic sermonic theory. This book is designed to help meet that deficiency.

The evangelistic sermon must be directed accurately toward the hearer and at life as it is being lived today. The evangelistic sermon must be aimed at convincing the hearer's mind, moving his feelings, and persuading his will to the point at which he will accept as his philosophy of life, "For to me to live is Christ, and to die is gain" (Phil. 1:21).

22. Raymond W. McLaughlin, *Communication for the Church*, p. 61.
23. Ralph L. Lewis, *Speech for Persuasive Preaching*, p. 89.

# I

## *Significance of the Holy Spirit in the Life of the Pulpit Evangelist*

THE HOLY SPIRIT is the evangelist's indispensable partner in the proclamation of the gospel of Christ. The scriptural analogies regarding the Holy Spirit speak to this point. In John 3 He is likened to wind that stirs. In Acts 2 He is likened to fire that purifies. In Isaiah 61 He is likened to oil that invigorates. In Revelation 22 He is likened to water that refreshes. The church today needs evangelistic preaching that will stir, purify, invigorate, and refresh the people of God.

Apart from the Spirit of God at work in his heart and life, the preacher's sermons will be echo chambers of meaningless words and irrelevant thoughts. The Holy Spirit is the "Divine Dynamic" who enables the evangelist to be powerful, persuasive, and practical. It is the "divine plus" of the Spirit that transforms mere speaking into masterful preaching. Under the direction of the Spirit of God, the evangelist becomes fully committed to the treasured reserves of the living Word of God. Moreover, he experiences liberty and a relaxed naturalness in delivery. But even more important, it is the Holy Spirit alone who can accomplish the aim of all evangelistic preaching, namely, a changed life. He is the generator of spiritual life. It is the Holy Spirit who cross-examines the sinner, showing him the error of his way (John 16:8-9). It is the Spirit of God who creates a hunger in the human heart for the righteousness of Christ that comes by faith (John 16:8, 10), and it is He who convinces lost men and women of a coming judgment because the "prince of this world is judged" (John 16:11).

In the final analysis, no sermonic method can become a substitute for the Spirit of God. Although the Spirit-empowered evangelist should know and use the tried and true principles of preaching that this book seeks to unfold, he must ever be mindful that there is no replacement for the personal presence of the third Person of the Trinity in his personal life or in his pulpit ministry. To preach in the energy of the flesh is utterly fruitless. Paul was well aware of this when he wrote to the Thessalonians, "For our gospel did not come to you in word only, but also in power and in the Holy Spirit and with full conviction" (1 Thess. 1:5, NASB). As ministers of the gospel, we dare not depend on natural means to produce supernatural results.

## A. The Place of the Holy Spirit in the Personal Life of the Pulpit Evangelist

The Holy Spirit is the calling agent of the church (Acts 13:2). He alone has the prerogative of appointing men to preach the glorious gospel of Christ. It was George Whitefield, the well-known evangelist of another decade, who held that any minister should be able to say before he undertakes to preach, "The Spirit of the Lord is upon me, because He hath anointed me to preach the gospel." Pastoral theologian Vinet explained, "We must be . . . called of God. A call to a ministry which is exercised in the name of God, and in which he is represented, can emanate only from him. The business here, in fact, is not our's, it is another's, and that other is God: . . . the call ought to be Divine."[1] A called man in contact with God is the first prerequisite for effective evangelistic preaching. As Arthur Hoyt observed nearly a century ago,

1. A. Vinet, *Pastoral Theology: Or the Theory of the Evangelical,* ed. and trans. Thomas H. Skinner, p. 76.

"The person of the preacher is the life of the sermon."

Not only does the Holy Spirit call, but He also equips. The Scriptures declare that it is the Holy Spirit who has given "gifted men" to the church, "some as apostles, and some as prophets, and some as evangelists, and some as pastors and teachers, for the equipping of the saints for the work of service, to the building up of the body of Christ" (Eph. 4:11-12, NASB). The evangelist, therefore, is one of the several channels the Spirit of God uses to accomplish His purposes in the lives of people. In addition, He superintends the distribution of spiritual ability as He wills (1 Cor. 12:11) so that the entire body of Christ will be edified (1 Cor. 12:7; 14:12) and Jesus Christ will be glorified (John 16:14).

Not only does the Holy Spirit call and equip the evangelist, but He also strengthens him for his monumental task. The Spirit of God enables the preacher to discipline his mind and his body. He prods the man of God to deeper devotional study and intercessory prayer. He helps him handle the multiplicity of demands on his time and energy that otherwise would inhibit and stunt his ministry and influence for Christ. Through the power of the Spirit at work within him, the preacher is able to overcome the ministerial temptations of pride, jealousy, self-conceit, covetousness, cowardice, and laziness (Rev. 2:17; 3:21). May the reminder the Lord gave to Zerubbabel ever be our motto in ministry: " 'Not by might nor by power, but by My Spirit,' says the LORD of hosts" (Zech. 4:6, NASB).

B. THE PLACE OF THE HOLY SPIRIT IN THE PRAYER LIFE
OF THE PULPIT EVANGELIST

It was the great evangelist C. H. Spurgeon who said,

> The minister who does not earnestly pray over his work must surely be a vain and conceited man. He acts as if he thought himself sufficient of himself, and therefore needed

19

not to appeal to God. Yet what a baseless pride to conceive that our preaching can ever be in itself so powerful that it can turn men from their sins and bring them to God without the working of the Holy Ghost.[2]

The Spirit-controlled evangelist will be preeminently a man of prayer. Paul reminded the Ephesians that prayer is the energy that enables the child of God to wear the whole armor of God and to wield the "sword of the Spirit, which is the word of God" (Eph. 6:17, NASB). As ministers of the gospel, we are encouraged to "pray at all times in the Spirit" (Eph. 6:18, NASB). That is to say, we are to pray under the guidance of the Spirit, in fellowship with the Spirit, and in dependence upon the Spirit. Such praying in the Spirit's power enables one to be in the will of God at all times (cf. Rom. 8:26-27).

Paul also equated dynamic personal prayer with powerful public utterance: "And pray on my behalf, that utterance may be given to me in the opening of my mouth, to make known with boldness the mystery of the gospel" (Eph. 6:19, NASB). Paul's confidence was not in himself. He recognized his need of help from heaven. Therefore, he encouraged others to stand with him in prayer so that the glad tidings of salvation could be sounded forth boldly from the gospel trumpet he was lifting to his lips.

E. M. Bounds drove home forcefully the need for prayer in his book *Power Through Prayer:*

> What the Church needs today is not more machinery or better, not new organizations or more and novel methods, but men whom the Holy Ghost can use—men of prayer, men mighty in prayer. The Holy Ghost does not flow through methods, but through men. He does not come on machinery, but on men. He does not anoint plans, but men—men of prayer.[3]

2. Charles H. Spurgeon, *Lectures to My Students*, p. 47.
3. E. M. Bounds, *Power Through Prayer*, p. 10.

20

## C. The Place of the Holy Spirit in the Pulpit Evangelist's Sermon Preparation

The intellectual and theological laziness exemplified by some evangelists in their sermon preparation is worthy of all the criticism it receives. Dr. Jowett was right when he observed, "Preaching that costs nothing accomplishes nothing. If the study is a lounge, the pulpit will be an impertinence."[4] Today, people need to have more than the fronts of their minds tickled with some interesting anecdote or emotional illustration. The Holy Spirit does not bless shoddy preparation, nor does He make up for it. To go into the pulpit as a representative of Christ without being thoroughly prepared casts a bad reflection not only upon the preacher, but also upon the Holy Spirit. The story is told of a preacher who began his sermon with an explanation, "I don't prepare—I just let the Bible flop open and let the Holy Spirit do the rest." After the message, he was greeted by an irate parishioner who said, "I didn't know the Holy Spirit was so boring and uninteresting." It is imperative, therefore, that the pulpit evangelist prepare as if there were no such Person as the Holy Spirit but preach as if there were no one but the Holy Spirit.

The strategic role of the Holy Spirit in the sermonizer's preparation is seen in the ministries He performs. First, the Holy Spirit is the *producer* of the evangelist's primary source material, the Word of God. The testimony of Scripture is clear: "All Scripture is inspired by God and profitable for teaching, for reproof, for correction, for training in righteousness; that the man of God may be adequate, equipped for every good work" (2 Tim. 3:16-17, NASB). The word *inspiration* literally means "God-breathed-out." Possibly a better word for inspiration would be *expiration*. Scripture is not to be thought of as already in existence when God subsequently breathed into it, but as being brought into existence by the breath, or Spirit, of God. The Scriptures are not of

4. J. H. Jowett, *The Preacher: His Life and Work*, p. 114.

21

human origin but were supernaturally communicated as God the Holy Spirit moved upon the biblical writers, prompting them to record with their own unique personalities and styles divine truth originating in the mind of God. The apostle Peter spoke of this: "But know this first of all, that no prophecy of Scripture is a matter of one's own interpretation, for no prophecy was ever made by an act of human will, but men moved by the Holy Spirit spoke from God" (2 Pet. 1:20-21, NASB). The Spirit of Truth (John 14:17) is the Author of Scripture. His reservoir of revealed truth can never be exhausted. As the sermonizer builds his life and ministry on the timeless principles divinely breathed out by the Spirit of God, he will always have sermonic material that is need oriented, people centered, and life transforming.

Second, the Holy Spirit is the *penetrator* of the evangelist's understanding, enabling him to properly observe, interpret, apply, and communicate gospel truth. The Spirit of Truth is the one who quickens the mind of the preacher, opening up to him the core truth revealed in the Word. Apart from the illumination of the Spirit of God, which comes as one prayerfully researches and reflects upon the text, no sermonic power is possible. The psalmist David prayed for divine enlightenment: "Open my eyes, that I may behold Wonderful things from Thy law" (Psalm 119:18, NASB). A model prayer for the illumination of the Spirit of God to quicken and deepen the understanding is found in Ephesians 1:17-19a:

> That the God of our Lord Jesus Christ, the Father of glory, may give to you a spirit of wisdom and of revelation in the knowledge of Him. I pray that the eyes of your heart may be enlightened, so that you may know what is the hope of His calling, what are the riches of the glory of His inheritance in the saints, and what is the surpassing greatness of His power toward us who believe (NASB).

Such a humbling of ourselves before God, acknowledging to

Him our darkness and appealing for His illumination, will not go unrewarded. Fresh life, light, and power from the Word will be a daily reality.

Third, the Holy Spirit is the *provider* of the evangelist's authority. People need more than an opinion from a preacher. "Thus says the Lord" is the voice from heaven that people long to hear. Apart from divine truth internalized through the indwelling presence and illumination of the Spirit of God, there is no authority in preaching. Apart from the Spirit's authority in the Word, all preaching is like "sounding brass" and "tinkling cymbals." Paul appealed to the Spirit's authority in explaining his preaching to the Corinthians: "My message and my preaching were not in persuasive words of wisdom, but in demonstration of the Spirit and of power, that your faith should not rest on the wisdom of men, but on the power of God" (1 Cor. 2:4-5, NASB; cf. 10-14). It does not matter who you are or what your position in the ministry may be. It is the authority of the Spirit and of the revealed Word of God that alone will bring power to the evangelistic proclamation.

A century ago William Arthur wrote, "If the preaching of the gospel is to exercise a great power over mankind, it must be either by enlisting extraordinary men or by endowing of ordinary men with extraordinary power."[5] Admittedly, there will never be enough outstanding men to go around. Most pulpits will be filled with just ordinary men with ordinary ability. The hope of the church is that God has endowed ordinary men in the past and will continue to endow ordinary men in the future, until the task of worldwide evangelization is complete. As God used an ordinary layman like D. L. Moody to turn America Godward in the latter part of the nineteenth century, so the Spirit of God can use each one today who will give Him his life and his talents. In so doing, the motto that

5. William Arthur, *The Tongue of Fire*, p. 67.

motivated Moody will again be instrumental in motivating men to be extraordinary men for God: "The world has yet to see what God will do with and for and through and in and by the man who is fully and wholly consecrated to Him. I will try my utmost to be that man."

# II

## Surveying the History of Evangelistic Preaching

To GAIN INSIGHT into the background to which contemporary American evangelistic preaching owes its impetus, it is profitable to survey the entire field of the history of preaching. Such a survey gives one an invaluable perspective. John Ker in his book *Lectures on the History of Preaching* listed several advantages that may be derived from such an investigation. One becomes acquainted with the most interesting and important men, events, and trains of thought that have been prominent in the Christian era. The condition of the Christian church and its impact upon contemporary culture become visible. The great themes of the Scriptures—God, the soul, eternity, sin, Christ, and salvation—are articulated skillfully by the great masters of the pulpit. One is able to perceive how they addressed themselves to the spirit of their times to become men above their times. Their homiletic faults are exposed, not in a derisive manner, but rather as a corrective to help succeeding generations of preachers avoid the paths that inhibted their total effectiveness. In addition, one will be reminded of the truth that whenever vital Christian truth has been presented toward the goal of meeting human needs, men have been found ready to listen. Finally, such a survey shows that all kinds of men can be useful as Christian ministers, provided they are true, earnest, and willing to learn.[1]

1. John Ker, *Lectures on the History of Preaching*, ed. A. R. Macewen, p. 12.

25

We are grouping revivalistic, soul-winning, evangelistic, and kerygmatic preaching under the general heading "evangelistic." Such preaching is proclaiming the gospel of Jesus Christ in such a way that men will repent of their sin by turning to Christ.

Since the major interest of this book is sermonic method, we have noted as accurately as possible the information provided by the authors we studied that would indicate the sermonic method employed by each evangelist herein described.[2]

The five canons of speech described in chapter 1 provided the basic structure for the gathering of material with reference to the sermonic method of evangelistic preachers.[3] The five canons are invention, or the discovery of ideas; arrangement, or the organization of ideas discovered; style, or the phrasing of ideas discovered and arranged; memory, or the retention of ideas discovered, arranged, and phrased; and delivery, meaning the presentation verbally and visually of ideas discovered, organized, phrased, and retained. Of these five canons, memory is omitted from this book because only one evangelist, Christmas Evans, is noted for his memory by the writers on the history of preaching.[4]

This chapter has four parts (corresponding to the four canons of speech), which in turn are each divided into eight historical segments in the history of preaching. The eight historical segments are:

| | | |
|---|---|---|
| The Patristic Age | A.D. | 70-430 |
| The Early Medieval Period | | 430-1095 |
| The Central Medieval Age | | 1095-1300 |

2. Appendix B contains a chronological listing of the most prominent preachers in the history of preaching who could be termed "evangelistic." In this chapter, only those preachers whose sermonic method is described by the authors we studied will be cited.
3. See Appendix A.
4. "Few men have had such an endless store of Scripture verses at instant command as he. In some of his sermons there are long paragraphs that are made up largely of proof-texts or portions of proof-texts. He could mingle these with his sermon with rare skill, supporting every sentence at times with one or more portions of a verse of Scripture" (F. R. Webber, *A History of Preaching in Britain and America*, 2:582).

| | |
|---|---|
| The Renaissance and Late Medieval Age | 1300-1500 |
| The Reformation Period | 1500-1572 |
| The Early Modern Period | 1572-1789 |
| The Late Modern Period | 1789-1900 |
| The Twentieth Century | 1900-Present |

Within the discussion of each historical segment is a chronological listing of evangelistic preachers and their noteworthy sermonic emphases as related to the five canons of speech. By this means, one can gain an overall historical perspective on evangelistic preaching that will help in gaining an appreciation for the great evangelists of the past.

## A. INVENTION

Among the five canons of classical rhetoric, invention is not only the first in time but also the first in importance. The careful evangelistic sermonizer will conduct much research and give much thought to the content of his message before taking the platform. Invention in this book includes such areas as text, subject, theme, functional elements (illustration and application), and sermonic method of preparation. The Bible is the basic handbook for evangelistic preaching; prayer is the primary method in sermon preparation; and a loving study of people is one of the best sources of ideas.

### THE PATRISTIC AGE (A.D. 70-430)

Writers on the history of preaching record that Chrysostom, or John of Antioch (347?-407), was also known as "The Golden Mouthed."[5] This great evangelistic preacher used an abundance of illustrative material and also had a remarkable ability to apply the principles of the Bible to the needs of his hearers.

### THE CENTRAL MEDIEVAL AGE (1095-1300)

Dominic (1170-1221) was deeply concerned for the conversion of heretics. As with Chrysostom, he was known for the

5. Edwin C. Dargan, *A History of Preaching*, 1:86.

functional element of illustration in his sermonic invention. Pattison, in his *History of Preaching,* stated that Dominic appealed to his audiences directly by using illustrations, anecdotes, fables, legends, and grotesque fancies. Moreover, he had the uncanny ability of telling stories of the torments of the lost and the glories of paradise that induced the desired and appropriate response in his hearers.

Anthony of Padua (1195?-1231) attracted such large crowds that no building could accommodate them. It is said that as many as thirty thousand people came at a time to hear him preach in the open air. His illustrative material was what made him outstanding as an evangelistic preacher. He drew his illustrations from the everyday life around him—from nature, people, the trades and occupations of his people, and from the habits of animals. Dargan paid him a great compliment when he said, "In drawing power he has never been surpassed, rivaled only by his fellow Franciscan Berthold, later in the century, and by Whitefield, perhaps Moody, and a few others, in modern times."[6]

The final preacher in the central medieval age whose methodology is discussed in writings on the history of preaching is Berthold of Regensburg (1220?-72?). Like Anthony of Padua, he was an open-air preacher. His evangelistic sermons, which were doctrinal, evidence his acquaintance with the church fathers and other theological literature. Repentance was his principal theme.

THE RENAISSANCE AND LATE MEDIEVAL AGE (1300-1500)

John Tauler of Strasburg (1290-1361) "pointed one and all to the Saviour, whom he himself found the only refuge from his own sins and from the evils of the times."[7] Not much is said of his method other than that his sermons were full of illustrations and that the applications of the religious prin-

6. Ibid., 1:256.
7. Ibid., 1:286.

ciples he proclaimed were tied in with homely duties for the ordinary man.

The founder of the Brethren of Common Life, Gerhard Groot (1349-84), was known as an evangelistic preacher because his subject matter centered on repentance and faith. Moreover, his ministry was blessed with many conversions and real amendment of life. In addition to those two prominent themes, Groot also made a concentrated effort to adapt his preaching to the needs of his people.

John Geiler of Kaisersberg (1445-1510), "the greatest German preacher of the popular type,"[8] is recognized as the one who aroused the German mind in preparation for the Reformation. He is known in the history of preaching as an evangelist who put much labor into the preparation of his sermons, reading widely and also closely observing human nature. He drew from many sources for timely and appropriate illustrations.

THE REFORMATION PERIOD (1500-72)

One of the greatest evangelistic preachers during this period was Hugh Latimer (1485?-1555), called "The Father of English preaching."[9] Said he, "Take away preaching and take away salvation. . . . Preaching is the thing the devil hath wrestled most against. This office of preaching is the only ordinary way which God hath appointed to save us all."[10] Salvation through Jesus Christ was his major theme. His sermons were soundly biblical, and he chose his subjects on the basis of people's needs. His applications were personal and his illustrations were at times crude. He preached without written preparation.

John Bradford (1510?-55) was an itinerant evangelist appointed by King Edward VI of England. Repentance was his favorite theme. As to subject matter, "He reproved sin sharp-

8. Ibid., 1:325.
9. Webber, 1:166.
10. T. H. Pattison, *The History of Christian Preaching*, p. 149.

ly, preached the grace of God sweetly, condemned heresy and error fearlessly and urged all to godly living."[11] He spent much time applying the truth to the lives of his hearers.

## THE EARLY MODERN PERIOD (1572-1789)

The Italian evangelist Paolo Segneri (1624-94) has been called the "restorer of sacred eloquence" and "the father of modern pulpit eloquence" in Italy.[12] He prepared his sermons carefully and based them on the foundation of a thorough study of the Word of God. His illustrations were drawn from observation and reading.

The evangelistic ministry of John Wesley (1703-91) spanned sixty-six years. During that time he preached forty-two thousand sermons. He preached to all kinds of crowds, large and small. His favorite preaching hour was five o'clock in the morning, because then the working people could gather to hear him before their work began. He proclaimed the forgotten doctrinal truth of his day, justification by faith. Wesley also stressed the inadequacy of the law to save.

Gilbert Tennent (1703-64) was active during the Great Awakening in America and was a traveling companion of George Whitefield on some of Whitfield's preaching missions in the colonies.

## THE LATE MODERN PERIOD (1789-1900)

Rowland Hill (1744-1833) "was a preacher of rare gifts, and his contemporaries are agreed that his manner, more than any other preacher, resembled that of Whitefield. He had the same evangelical fervor, the same love for souls, and much of Whitefield's superior gift of oratory."[13] He had great illustrative ability.

The diligent preaching of Richard Moore (1762-1841)

11. Webber, 1:187.
12. Dargan, 2:43.
13. Webber, 1:425.

30

helped to save the American Episcopal Church from total collapse.[14]

Christmas Evans (1766-1838) was called the "Golden-Mouthed Chrysostom of Wales."[15] The greatest of all Welsh preachers, Evans usually preached seventeen times a week, five times on Sunday and twice on each weekday. He preached often on evangelistic subjects.

It was said of Leigh Richmond's (1772-1827) preaching that almost every sermon had salvation for its theme. His Christocentric message was illustrated with the scenes of everyday life.

John Angell James (1785-1859) was an outstanding evangelistic preacher. Joseph Parker said of him: "Probably few men have by the grace of God converted more souls than the Rev. Angell James. Account for it as we may, his preaching was always attended with profound spiritual effects. . . . He reaped a harvest second to none since apostolic days."[16] James began his sermon preparation by studying the biblical text in great detail. After carefully exegeting the text, he would make striking personal applications to the daily lives of his hearers. This careful weaving of the text with appropriate applications must account for much of his sermonic power. He could exegete for sermonic use any portion of the Old or New Testaments.

The evangelistic efforts of Nathaniel Taylor (1786-1858) helped account for four revivals that broke out during his ten years as pastor of the First Church of New Haven, Connecticut. On one night during such a revival there were seventy professions of faith in Christ. He preached on the characteristic evangelistic themes. He also believed strongly that the exposition of doctrine must be backed by an application of that truth to the lives of the hearers.

Charles G. Finney (1792-1875) "maintained a dignified type of preaching, presenting sin and salvation in a manner

14. Ibid., 3:159.
15. Ibid., 2:585.
16. Ibid., 1:468.

31

that suggests the trained attorney rather than the revivalist."[17] He laid stress on the deity of Christ, His vicarious atonement, justification by grace through faith, the transforming power of the Holy Spirit, the justice of God's moral government, the progressive revelation of God's will, sanctification, and millennialism. He also spoke out against such vices as drunkenness, gambling, fighting, and cheating. His illustrations were drawn from the everyday occurrences of life—farming, mechanics, and other prominent vocational crafts.

Ludwig Hofacker (1798-1828) was a German evangelist whose sermons were addressed primarily to non-Christians; he paid little attention to the nurture of believers.

Of evangelist Charles Spurgeon (1834-92) it was said, "He was doubtless the most impressive and permanently successful evangelistic preacher of his age."[18] He knew how to gather material rapidly, and he used biblical data in a rich and effective manner.

Dwight L. Moody (1837-99) had a unique way of preparing his sermons. He kept his sermon notes in a large manila envelope on which the title of the intended message was written. Then, as he collected poems, stories, or other sources of thoughts, he would slip them into the envelope until he had collected enough material for a sermon. "The result was a hodgepodge of illustrations and texts all reiterating one simple idea over and over again."[19] Moody's great theme was the love of God. Another theme was premillennialism. His illustrations were characterized, among other things, by deeply moving deathbed stories.

Frederick B. Meyer (1847-1929) won fame in four different fields of activity: "as an evangelist, as an expert in spiritual therapy, as a crusader and as a prolific author."[20]

17. Ibid., 3:320.
18. Dargan, 2:537.
19. William G. J. McLoughlin, *Modern Revivalism: Charles G. Finney to Billy Graham*, p. 244.
20. Webber, 1:643.

The final evangelistic preacher of the late modern age whose sermonic method relates to invention is Samuel P. Jones (1847-1906), who was called the "Moody of the South."[21] He emphasized the great social aspects of Christianity. His illustrations were homely.

## THE TWENTIETH CENTURY (1900-PRESENT)

B. Fay Mills (1857-1916) preached primarily "a doctrine of social responsibility and social action."[22] This was in marked contrast to his early activity, in which he had preached personal repentance and conversion. He was praised by Washington Gladden as an exponent of the "new evangelism" (social gospel). This identification is supported by some of his sermon titles: "Evils in Material Conditions," "Educational Defects," "Business Sins," "Political Sins," "The Christianization of Business," "The Regeneration of Politics," "The Salvation of Society," and "The Moral Influence of the Public School."

An ex-baseball star turned evangelist describes William A. (Billy) Sunday (1863-1935). He was the first evangelist to carry a staff of workers with him. Sunday claimed to have spoken to one hundred million people in the days before radio and public address systems. Heaven and hell were his major concerns, and he crusaded against sin in a manner that Jonathan Edwards might have envied. He also spoke out against social abuses of his time—big business, slum housing, and oppressive labor conditions.

The radio evangelist of the International Lutheran Hour, Walter A. Maier (1893-1950), is said to have preached to thirty-six million people by radio. He spoke out against sin as few men in the history of preaching have done.

The name of William Franklin (Billy) Graham (b. 1918) is very familiar to Americans. He has preached to more people than any other evangelist in the history of preaching. His great

21. McLoughlin, p. 282.
22. Ibid., p. 336.

emphasis is on repentance from sin: he has also preached social reform, but that has always been subordinate to the gospel of Christ. His ability to relate and apply what is happening nationally and internationally to the Scriptures has been of great benefit to his ministry.

## B. Arrangement

Arrangement, according to Isocrates, one of the principal figures in Greek rhetoric, consists of four parts, namely, proem (introduction), narrative, proof, and epilogue. The necessity of careful arrangement was noted by John Genung: "The discourse is to be not a mere agglomeration of statements, but an organism, fitted to move as one thought, and to be incorporated into the reader's mind."[23] Arrangement here will be concerned with what the writers on the history of preaching recorded regarding the introduction, proposition, body, and conclusion of the evangelistic sermon.

### THE CENTRAL MEDIEVAL AGE (1095-1300)

Bernard of Clairvaux (1091-1153) was a prominent French preacher who made his mark in life as a "theologian, mystic, man of affairs, partisan, crusade evangelist, and popular preacher."[24] His sermons were carefully prepared and evidenced the systematizing tendencies of Scholastic thought and method. Several writers have pointed out that his sermons were characterized by marked divisions.

Anthony of Padua was known as the "Friend of the Poor" and "The Thunder from on High."[25] Broadus said that Anthony was the first preacher to make a careful division of his sermons into several heads, or main points. For example, speaking on the text "Blessed are the dead which die in the Lord" (Rev. 14:13), Anthony proposed three things: (1) the

23. Lester Thonssen, ed., *Selected Readings in Rhetoric and Public Speaking*, p. 313.
24. Dargan, 1:208.
25. Pattison, p. 108.

Debt of Nature—"the dead"; (2) the Merit of Grace—"who die in the Lord"; and (3) the Reward of Glory—"blessed."[26] These formal structural divisions led Dargan to conclude that Anthony "did a service to preaching in popularizing a better structure of discourse than that of the homily."[27] Moreover, Pattison noted, "He kept very close to the words of his text in the division of his subject."[28]

Berthold of Regensburg followed the clear arrangement of the Scholastics in his sermons. He amplified the main divisions of his sermons by employing imagery, homely illustrations, and vivid dialogues.

## THE RENAISSANCE AND LATE MEDIEVAL AGE (1300-1500)

According to Dargan, the greatest preacher among the mystics of the Renaissance period was John Tauler of Strasburg. His sermonic arrangement reverted to the loose form of the homily, which had lost popularity because of the Scholastic influence, and the formal sermonic division of such men as Bernard of Clairvaux, Anthony of Padua, and Berthold of Regensburg, who thrived during the central medieval age.

John Geiler of Kaisersberg is known for his simple sermonic arrangement, in which he drew comparisons and lessons from the text and from daily life. His main divisions were very numerous and lengthy, thus being difficult to remember.

## THE REFORMATION PERIOD (1500-72)

Only one of the evangelistic preachers during this period is noted for his sermonic arrangement, John Bradford. His sermonic introductions were simple and natural, not complex and forced. Then too, Bradford's introductions were brief and to the point. His separation of the biblical text into logical divisions is noteworthy. In his sermon on Matthew 4:17, "Repent: for the kingdom of heaven is at hand," he spoke of

26. John A. Broadus, *Lectures on the History of Preaching*, p. 103.
27. Dargan, 1:256.
28. Pattison, p. 109.

repentance as consisting of three elements: (1) a genuine sorrow in view of sin; (2) some persuasion or hope of God's willingness to pardon sin for Christ's sake; and (3) a purpose to amend and turn to God. His subdivision for point 1 consisted of the motives to sorrow for sin; for point 2, the tokens of God's willingness to forgive; for point 3, the results of a true purpose to amend.[29] His sermon on the Lord's Supper had three divisions in the form of questions: (1) Who instituted this sacrament? (2) What was instituted? (3) To what end was it instituted? His elaboration of these main points was logical and concise.[30]

### THE EARLY MODERN PERIOD (1572-1789)

Richard Baxter (1615-91) was also greatly influenced by the Scholastic method of dividing and subdividing his sermons. He endeavored to "milk" the text of its contents in an analytical manner. His divisions were characterized by minuteness.

Paolo Segneri employed rhetorical questions with great effectiveness in his introductions. Furthermore, his introductions evidenced much study on his part and logical argument. The logical progression of thought that commenced with the introduction was carried on throughout the discourse.

John Bunyan (1628-88) was an outstanding evangelist whose sermonic arrangement was clear, logical, and analytical.

John Wesley, in the mind of Pattison, arranged his thoughts admirably. "To systematize was as natural with him as to breathe. He spoke, as he lived, by rule."[31] In the introduction to his famous sermon "The Great Assize" (text: Rom. 14:10), Wesley began in the secular and built toward the major thrust of his text. From there he moved smoothly to the following three main points: (1) the chief circumstances that will pre-

29. Dargan, 1:501.
30. Webber, 1:189.
31. Pattison, p. 257.

cede our standing before the judgment seat of Christ; (2) the judgment itself; and (3) a few of the circumstances that will follow it. The conclusion to the sermon was largely a forceful application of these main points to the various classes represented in his listening audience and an exhortation to come to repentance.[32]

## THE LATE MODERN PERIOD (1789-1900)

The Swiss evangelist Johann Caspar Lavater (1741-1801) was remembered for his "warmth of heart, earnestness of soul, richness of fancy, clearness and vigor of thought, and force yet variety of style."[33] His sermonic arrangement included a good exposition of the text and an application after each main division.

Rowland Hill arranged his sermons into main divisions and subdivisions, which were characterized by logical progression.

Christmas Evans was known as a great "two-point" evangelistic preacher.[34] His introductions were brief, and his main divisions were expressed in as few words as possible. The accompanying subdivisions were logical and progressive, building to a great climax.

Klause Harms (1778-1855), the great evangelistic preacher from northern Germany, was not expository, but his divisions were almost always clear and striking.

John Angell James always concluded his message by inviting people to come to Christ. His conclusion worked smoothly into his invitation. The sermons of Nathaniel Taylor were well ordered.

The "national dean of evangelists"[35] was Charles G. Finney. His sermons were arranged logically, and the conclusions were carefully planned, appealing for a changed life.

"The greatest Baptist preacher of the Nineteenth Century"

32. Dargan, 2:323-24.
33. Ibid., 2:232.
34. Webber, 2:582.
35. McLoughlin, p. 17.

was Charles Spurgeon, who pastored the six-thousand-seat Metropolitan Tabernacle in London.[36] His sermonic arrangement was often homiletically faulty and careless, although in his unhurried moments he preferred a clear division of his subject based on the words of the text. His hasty sermonic preparation was evidenced by a lack of clear-cut arrangement.

Dwight L. Moody would begin his sermonic preparation with a theme. He would look up all the references concerning that theme in *Cruden's Concordance* and then seek to tie all the verses together into some meaningful order. In his conclusions, which were heavy in application, he sought to drive home the theme with present-day relevance.

THE TWENTIETH CENTURY (1900-PRESENT)

Reuben A. Torrey (1856-1928), through logical arrangement, built up his sermons to a great climax.

J. Wilbur Chapman (1859-1918) arranged his sermons around numerous sentimental stories centered upon some theme. The sermons reached their climax in an appeal to the best in man or the love of mother, home, or country. It has been said that one audience counted seventeen such stories in one half-hour address.

McLoughlin, in his *Modern Revivalism: Charles G. Finney to Billy Graham,* mentioned the way the evangelists of the twentieth century tied their conclusions in with their invitations. B. Fay Mills used decision cards in his invitations. Billy Sunday used the same approach to some extent. However, his invitations to come forward were so loosely phrased that they lacked any real religious content. Billy Graham is also adept at concluding his sermon with a call for converts.

C. STYLE

The derivation of the word *style* is discussed in "Sermon

36. Dargan, 2:534-536.

Style in Contemporary Terms" in *Baker's Dictionary of Practical Theology*:

> The word style comes from the Latin *stylus,* which referred to the pointed iron pen with which the Romans wrote on their tablets. Style is one's manner of expressing thought whether in writing or in speaking. It is the expression in language of the thought, qualities, and spirit of the man. It is his characteristic way of expressing his thoughts. It involves the use of the right words in the right places. Style is the manner, as distinguished from the matter.[37]

Robert T. Oliver, in his definitive work *The Psychology of Persuasive Speech,* observed, "The persuasive effect of sheer stylistic excellence is tremendous. 'Give me the right word,' wrote Joseph Conrad, 'and the right accent and I will move the world.' "[38] In this section the nature, improvement, and quality of evangelistic style are noted.

### THE PATRISTIC AGE (A.D. 70-430)

Chrysostom has the unique distinction of being known chiefly as "the prince of expository preachers," but he is also known as an evangelist in that he lashed out against the sin and corruption of his day. Broadus commented on his style:

> As to style he certainly ranges the whole gamut of expression; for while his style is generally elevated, often magnificent, and sometimes extravagant, it occasionally becomes homely and rough as he lays bare the follies and vices of men.[39]

### THE CENTRAL MEDIEVAL AGE (1095-1300)

The words of Broadus concerning the style of Bernard of Clairvaux cannot be improved upon:

37. Lloyd M. Perry, "Sermon Style in Contemporary Terms," in *Baker's Dictionary of Practical Theology,* ed. Ralph G. Turnbull, p. 74.
38. Robert T. Oliver, *The Psychology of Persuasive Speech,* p. 244.
39. Broadus, p. 79.

His style has an elegant simplicity and sweetness that is charming, and while many of his expressions are as striking as those of Augustine, they seem perfectly easy and natural. His utterance and gesture are described as in the highest degree impressive, his power of persuasion was felt by high and low to be something irresistible.[40]

## THE REFORMATION PERIOD (1500-72)

Only one evangelistic preacher during this period is noted for his style by the writers in the field of the history of preaching. His name is Hugh Latimer, and his unique style is best evidenced in his sermon entitled "Sermon of the Plough." Pattison called it the finest specimen of Latimer's style—simple, enthusiastic, and conversational. Moreover, his style reflected an inexhaustible supply of homely and effective humor.

## THE EARLY MODERN PERIOD (1572-1789)

The preaching style of Richard Baxter was "rough and careless" and at the same time pleasing and expressive. In addition, it was characterized by simplicity and clarity.

The style of Paolo Segneri was described by Dargan as "lofty, diffuse, highly wrought, intense; but while lacking flexibility and ease, it so far surpasses in directness and power the overwrought manner of the time as by contrast to seem simple and severe."[41]

The magnificent style of John Bunyan has been described in great detail by the historians of preaching. Pattison readily pointed out that he had "an incomparable style: the noblest and purest Saxon ever used in the pulpit, and an imagination which places him beside Dante and Milton."[42] John Broadus commented: "He abounds in lively terms and racy phrases, in a vivid dramatism that no preacher has surpassed, and his homeliest expressions are redeemed from vulgarity

40. Ibid., p. 98.
41. Dargan, 2:44.
42. Pattison, p. 194.

by a native elegance, an instinctive good taste."[43] Pattison concluded:

> What Macaulay says of Bunyan as the author is equally true of Bunyan as the preacher: "No writer has said more exactly what he meant to say. For magnificence, for pathos, for vehement exhortation, for subtle disquisition, for every purpose of the poet and orator and the divine, the homely dialect is perfectly sufficient."[44]

Many of the key evangelists during the Great Awakening, such as Wesley, Tennent, and Whitefield, were remembered for their style. John Wesley was direct in his style and made no effort to be humorous. Pathos was also lacking, but he made up for those deficiencies with sound biblical exposition. Gilbert Tennent, an American immigrant from Ireland, was known for his flowery and diffuse style, which was characterized by warmth and urgency. George Whitefield (1714-70) was a great open-air evangelist in the United States and England. His style was simple and easily understood.

THE LATE MODERN PERIOD (1789-1900)

Christmas Evans, the "Poet of the Pulpit,"[45] had great descriptive and imaginative power that captivated his listeners. Along with his creative imagination, he combined passion and humor. Webber summarized: "He was a man of lively imagination. He was not content to tell a Bible story. He dramatized it, describing minutely the appearance of those of whom he spoke. If authentic detail was lacking, his lively Celtic imagination supplied it readily enough."[46]

The style of Charles G. Finney was conversational.

Dargan described the style of Charles Spurgeon as "rich, racy, homely, powerful Saxon—sometimes undignified, but

43. Broadus, p. 208.
44. Pattison, p. 194.
45. Ibid., p. 275.
46. Webber, 2:580.

41

ever clear and strong, and often sweet and eloquent."[47] Pattison said of him:

> In his early years he was often exceedingly eloquent, with an impetuous rush of words which subsequent experience, and perhaps suffering, toned down. The measured strength and sweetness of his tones in his later sermons became monotonous, and to break up the uniform harmony of his style he read Carlyle.[48]

Dwight L. Moody had a natural and often sentimental preaching style. He had the ability to move his audience from tears to laughter with surprising ease and rapidity. His way with words was seasoned with humor. "His sermons were made up of short, simple sentences, colloquial rhythms and idioms, blunt, almost earthy, forthrightness, and a lively sense of rustic humor," McLoughlin said.[49]

Frederick B. Meyer had a style that suggested the ornate, that is, the elaborate and flowery style of gifted rhetoricians.

The fiery style of Samuel P. Jones, the fearless American evangelist, was direct and tempered to the makeup of his audience. His sermons were known for their wit, invective, homespun philosophy, and satirical humor.

### THE TWENTIETH CENTURY (1900-PRESENT)

The historian McLoughlin, commenting on the style of Billy Sunday, said that it was characterized by slang. "Sunday justified his slang with the explanation, 'I want to reach the people so I use the people's language.' "[50] McLoughlin went on to say, "Slangy humor and florid rhetoric" were two of the basic ingredients of Sunday's style. The "sensational" style of Sunday is further seen in his mimicry and hyphenated series of expletives, which made up a large part of his repertoire.

Billy Graham, while in Korea in 1973, preached to over one

47. Dargan, 2:538.
48. Pattison, p. 337.
49. McLoughlin, p. 241.
50. Ibid., p. 429.

million people in a single service.[51] According to McLoughlin, his style in some ways is similar to Billy Sunday's. "Like
Billy Sunday, he told biblical stories in a slangy vernacular,
describing the prophet Amos as a 'hillbilly preacher' and saying that the unfaithful of Noah's day thought of him as 'an old
crazy fellow' with a 'screw loose somewhere.' "[52]

## D. Delivery

Delivery is primarily concerned with the presentation, both
visually and verbally, of the evangelistic message. Aristotle
defined delivery succinctly:

> The art of delivery has to do with the voice: with the right
> management of it to express each several emotion—as when
> to use a loud voice, when a soft, and when the intermediate;
> with the mode of using pitch—high, low, and intermediate;
> and with the rhythms to be used in each particular case.
> These are, in fact, the three things that receive attention:
> volume, modulation of pitch, and rhythm.[53]

Effective evangelistic delivery has often made the difference
between a mediocre and an eloquent address. Delivery in this
section is concerned with the psychological, visual, and audible factors involved in evangelistic preaching. Careful attention is also given to whether the evangelists listed by the historians of preaching spoke extemporaneously or read from
manuscripts.

THE PATRISTIC AGE (A.D. 70-430)

Chrysostom was an evangelistic preacher whose delivery
was powerful and effective. Pattison quoted Dr. Macgilvray
on this characteristic:

> As he advanced from exposition to illustration, from scrip-
> tural principle to practical appeals, his delivery became

---

51. See "Epochal Event: What God Did in Korea," *Christianity Today* 17:
    1009-10.
52. McLoughlin, p. 500.
53. Lane Cooper, *The Rhetoric of Aristotle*, p. 183.

gradually more rapid, his countenance more animated, his voice more vivid and intense. The people began to hold their breath. The joints of their loins were loosened. A creeping sensation like that produced by a series of electric waves passed over them. They felt as if drawn forwards toward the pulpit by a sort of magnetic influence. Some of those who were sitting rose from their seats; others were overcome with a kind of faintness as if the preacher's mental force were sucking the life out of their bodies, and by the time the discourse came to an end the great mass of that spellbound audience could only hold their heads and give vent to their emotion in tears.[54]

## THE CENTRAL MEDIEVAL AGE (1095-1300)

The basic appeal of Bernard of Clairvaux was for people to repent of their sins. Often he would call for a show of hands from those who wished to be restored to fellowship with God or the church. The delivery of Berthold of Regensburg was smooth and audibly clear in comparison to that of many mystics of his age.

## THE REFORMATION PERIOD (1500-72)

Several writers in the field of homiletic history were impressed with the delivery of Hugh Latimer. He was fearless in delivery and did not hesitate to adapt his preaching to the people in his congregation. He spoke "in a vivid, racy manner, with an occasional flash of wit, but always clear, direct and strong in his convictions."[55] He also was one of the few preachers to have used visual aids from the pulpit. Pattison related:

> His honest soul revolted against the tricks of popery. At St. Paul's he exhibited from the pulpit a certain image called the Rood of Grace; and the contemptible jugglery by which the pulling of concealed cords made it roll its eyes,

54. Pattison, p. 71.
55. Webber, 1:164.

shake its head, open or shut its mouth, was plainly exposed to the congregation.[56]

His delivery was also characterized by earnestness.

William Farel (1489-1565) had a successful evangelistic career in the towns of French Switzerland. His delivery was known for its persuasiveness.

## THE EARLY MODERN PERIOD (1572-1789)

Richard Baxter was known for his vehement earnestness in delivery. Said Webber, "So eloquent were his appeals to the consciences of his hearers that he fired his growing congregation with zeal for the cause. . . . Few men have ever equalled him in persuasiveness and in urgency of appeal."[57] Furthermore, Baxter wrote out his sermons but did not spend time revising them.

Paolo Segneri preached with a genuine fervor and interest in his hearers. He also displayed keen eagerness in presenting his message.

The tireless zeal with which John Bunyan carried on his evangelistic ministry is noted by the historians. His delivery was sincere and sympathetic.

The modern evangelistic method of reaching the masses probably received its impetus from the Jesuit priest Jacques Bridaine (1701-67). He used processions, choruses, banners, and the like to attract and impress large crowds. He also sought the approval and cooperation of other parish priests in his endeavors. Bridaine called for "public avowals of renewed faith or of first confessions of Christ."[58] Dargan described his great ability to "capture the crowd." Such an ability was evidenced by "sympathy with people of all kinds, knowledge of their real wants, simplicity and directness of language and argument, imagination and power of portraiture,

56. Pattison, p. 154.
57. Webber, 1:249-50.
58. Dargan, 2:255.

dramatic effect, occasional 'flights' of eloquence, fervor and earnestness of appeal."[59] For example, it is said that on one occasion when he was speaking on death, Bridaine had his congregation follow him to a nearby cemetery, where he made his closing appeal from a tomb.

John Wesley had a calm delivery, with a subdued intensity and glow that powerfully moved his listeners. His voice and his gestures were not dramatic, but he did evince a "fearless spirit," "intense earnestness," and "rare spiritual fervor."[60] Webber said of his delivery:

> His voice was so clear and penetrating that he could be heard by outdoor congregations of 30,000 people. He refrained from shouting, he was not dramatic, and he seldom made use of illustrations. No matter how turbulent his hearers might be, Wesley was always calm. He spoke in an animated conversational tone audible to the farthest fringe of the congregation.[61]

The delivery of George Whitefield, who had struggled against the call to preach, impressed by its effectiveness nearly all the writers on the history of preaching. It was characterized by "boldness and directness, intense earnestness, pathos and feeling, perfect action, a powerful and sonorous utterence, and a singular faculty of description. . . . As he preached, tears often rolled down his cheeks and fell upon the open Bible before him."[62] Dargan said of his delivery:

> There was evident sincerity and sympathy and goodwill which won the hearer at once; there was the high and subtle quality of soul which we call magnetism; there was intensity, sometimes passionate fervor, of earnestness which was often a veritable storm; there was a charm and grace of aspect and action, natural, winsome, irresistible; and with all this a

59. Ibid., 2:256.
60. Pattison, p. 258.
61. Webber, 1:345.
62. Ibid., 1:360-61.

voice of marvelous volume, penetration and harmony. His splendid imagination and dramatic power were controlled, and therefore really heightened in effect, by the loftiness of his aim and the evident unselfishness of his appeals.[63]

Pattison described his powerful quality of voice:

A voice rich and varied, an organ, a flute, a harp, all in one, and of such range that Franklin found by actual measurement that it could be distinctly heard by more than thirty thousand people; such exquisite modulation that it was said he could pronounce even the word "Mesopotamia" so as to move you to laughter or touch you to tears; gestures which never failed to express his thought, and an emotional nature which while never carrying him beyond himself would find vent in loud and passionate weeping. No one better understood the art of startling his hearers by an unexpected turn to his words.[64]

He also was known to use pauses effectively to emphasize significant words or phrases.

THE LATE MODERN PERIOD (1789-1900)

The great Swiss gospel preacher Johann Casper Lavater was known for his warm and earnest delivery and his clarity and vigor of thought. He preached extemporaneously and did not write out his sermons prior to delivering them.

Rowland Hill was said to have resembled the preaching model of George Whitefield. He had the same voluminous voice and much of the same dramatic quality. It was said that he could lead his congregation up Mt. Sinai and from there to Mount Calvary. He was a careful student of the text and preached extemporaneously.

Salvation was the theme of almost every message evangelist Leigh Richmond preached. He preached without notes and spoke in animated language. His appeals were directed toward

63. Dargan, 2:313.
64. Pattison, p. 269.

the heart and conscience. His audiences were constantly made aware of man's sin and the remedy provided by the cross.

Evangelist Jabez Bunting (1779-1858) has been characterized by some historians as one of the most remarkable men produced by the Methodist Church. His delivery was persuasive and powerful. He had the ability to arouse the indifferent, and his vivid descriptions of the wrath of God were said to have almost rivaled those of Jonathan Edwards. Urgency was also an important facet of his delivery.

John Angell James wrote out his evangelistic sermons entirely but then preached without notes unless under unusual circumstances. He was gifted with fluency of speech and excelled in preaching his sermons extemporaneously. However, he did not allow that natural strength to interfere with his thorough study of the text before entering the pulpit.

The evangelistic preaching of Nathaniel Taylor won wide acceptance. He specialized in exposition of doctrine and in the appeal for a changed life on the basis of sound biblical preaching. Taylor insisted that it is not enough merely to preach sin and grace. Such preaching must be accompanied by an urgent plea to the hearers to repent of their sins and make a decision for their Savior. His audible delivery impressed Webber: "He had a rich, sonorous voice, and was capable of flights of eloquence that awakened the admiration of friend and opponent alike."[65]

Charlès G. Finney, known for his famous "anxious bench"—where the sinner could come and hear the Word more directly, be made the subject of the prayers of the saints, and sometimes be conversed with individually—was an urgent, forceful evangelist. His motives, or appeals, in delivery were appeals to fear, to reasonableness, to the propriety of God's claims, to the hatefulness of sin, and to the stability of God's truth. He did not advocate emotionalism for the sake of emotion and was opposed totally to manuscript messages, which,

65. Webber, 3:222.

he believed, only impede the natural flow of content, emotions, and gestures.

German evangelist Ludwig Hofacker was known as the "true evangelist."[66] His delivery was characterized by thoroughness and genuine simplicity.

The delivery of Charles Spurgeon was free, easy, natural, and seasoned with humor. He spoke extemponaneously and often revised his sermons just before delivering them. But the strength of Spurgeon was his voice. Pattison noted, "His voice was a powerful organ. Its first note, while it filled with ease the largest room, was so personal that each one of his hearers seemed to be specially addressed. Without effort he could reach as many as twenty thousand persons."[67]

Lay evangelist Dwight L. Moody possessed a contagious earnestness that gripped the audience. Moreover, his delivery was simple but tender. Often he would weep for people to come to Christ. His gestures were few but emphatic. In his opening sermon in Brooklyn in 1875, "Speaking at the rate of 220 words per minute, he portrayed the battle of Jericho in vigorous language, hardly glancing at the notes held in the center of his Bible with an elastic band."[68]

Gifted evangelist F. B. Meyer was known to make "direct appeals to his hearers to forsake all things that might stand in the way of a complete acceptance of Jesus Christ as their Saviour."[69]

Samuel P. Jones had an unorthodox delivery. His gestures were vigorous, to say the least. He would wave his arms and point his finger repeatedly at his audience. On warm nights he often would remove his coat and speak in shirt sleeves.

THE TWENTIETH CENTURY (1900-PRESENT)

Amzi C. Dixon (1854-1925) was called in 1911 to the pul-

66. Dargan, 2:404.
67. Pattison, p. 335.
68. McLoughlin, p. 242.
69. Webber, 1:643.

pit of the Metropolitan Tabernacle in London, the pulpit made famous by Charles Spurgeon. Although his delivery was not sensational and he did not employ many of the popular revivalistic methods, Dixon did give people a chance to meet him after each service to make some kind of decision on the basis of the message preached. The tonal quality of his voice was his strength. Said Webber,

> Even when he denounced sin he never did it in a tone of sharp reproof. His words were emphatic, he painted sin in its blackest colors, he held out not the slightest hope for the unrepentant sinner, yet he did it all in a tone of voice that suggested a friend coming with an urgent warning.[70]

The delivery of Reuben A. Torrey was vehement, assertive, and intense. His voice was strong and could be heard with ease by fifteen to twenty thousand people. He did not mince words, and no one ever left his meeting with the slightest doubt about what the preacher had said.

Dwight L. Moody described J. Wilbur Chapman in 1895 as "the greatest evangelist in the country."[71] The tone of Chapman's delivery was pleading and friendly.

B. Fay Mills, a close associate of Chapman, preached his evangelistic messages without notes. Spontaneity was the fruit of such an approach. His delivery was simple, and his preaching tone was gentle, urgent, and pleading without being offensive or harsh.

The delivery of Billy Sunday has been long remembered and widely talked about. One word could sum it up—action! At times he would pace back and forth across the platform. On other occasions he would sling off his coat or stand on a chair. McLoughlin summarized his delivery with the following statements:

> The drama of the performance was heightened by his pound-

70. Ibid., 1:657-58.
71. McLoughlin, p. 377.

ing the pulpit, standing on a chair, swinging a chair over his head, sliding, jumping, falling, staggering, whirling, and even doing handsprings on the 30 foot platform. At the conclusion of his more dramatic sermons he would jump on top of the pulpit and vigorously wave an American flag.[72]

McLoughlin also said concerning Sunday's style:

He spoke at the rate of three hundred words per minute, but his sentences were short and simple, and he acted out every word he uttered so that those who did not hear it could see it. Like any experienced showman he knew how to draw laughter or applause, how to wait for it, and when to repeat a line or vary it slightly a second time in order to wring the full response from it.[73]

Walter A. Maier was known for his animated delivery, which was in marked contrast to the sledgehammer delivery techniques of his predecessors. His animation was grounded in intense conviction, which expressed itself in ways other than shouting.

The present-day delivery of Billy Graham is also characterized by animation and spontaneity. In addition, Graham considers fear to be a legitimate motive in evangelism.

From this survey of evangelistic sermonic method through the history of preaching, the following conclusions can be drawn:[74]

1. No evangelistic preacher, so far as the writers in the field of the history of preaching are concerned, has been known for his prowess in all five canons of classical rhetoric.

2. Only one evangelistic preacher, Christmas Evans, was known for his excellence in the canon of memory.

3. Seven evangelistic preachers, namely, Paolo Segneri, John Wesley, Charles G. Finney, Charles Spurgeon, Dwight

72. Ibid., p. 426.
73. Ibid.
74. See Appendix A.

51

L. Moody, Billy Sunday, and Billy Graham have excelled in invention, arrangement, style, and delivery. Christmas Evans was remembered for his invention, arrangement, style, and memory.

4. During the early medieval period, seven evangelists were known as "missionary preachers."[75] However, the writers on the history of preaching record nothing regarding their sermonic technique as it relates to the five canons of classical rhetoric. The reason for this is that after the death of Augustine in the early fifth century, the quality of preaching began to decline significantly and remained in a deplorable state until the twelfth century. That period can be termed the dark ages of preaching, as the clergy were corrupt and sermons were textless and showed little or no thought. Doctrine was not stressed and, apart from the circuit-riding missionary preachers, the period would have been even darker with respect to the preaching of a genuine gospel.

5. Beginning with the central medieval age and continuing through the Reformation period, there seems to have been an emphasis on invention among evangelistic preachers. During the central medieval age there was a revival of preaching, although the preaching was, in some cases, based on forced exegesis and too allegorical. The errors were gradually corrected, however, and the strong biblical content that characterized the Reformation took hold. On the other hand, A. T. Pierson noted that the main weakness of the Reformation was its failure to revive the evangelistic activity, although there was a renewal of evangelical faith.[76]

6. In the early modern period there appears to have been a sharp shift in evangelistic sermonic technique from invention and arrangement to style and delivery. There is a strong indication that the presentation of the evangelistic sermon took

75. See Appendix B.
76. Arthur T. Pierson, *Evangelistic Work in Principle and Practice*, pp. 104-5.

precedence over the preparation of the sermon during the time of the Great Awakening. It is significant that most of the great evangelists were engaged in itinerant evangelism; their traveling limited their time for sermonic preparation. In addition, writers on the history of preaching observe that John Wesley was the first evangelistic preacher to use conversational tone in his delivery.

7. The weakness of evangelists in the early modern period in invention and arrangement seems to have been corrected in the late modern period. That may have been because of the rise of rationalism, which necessitated that evangelistic preachers base their messages on the objective foundation of the Word of God. Invention, the discovery of ideas, and delivery, the presentation of those ideas, seem to have been stressed equally by notable evangelists.

8. The twentieth century has witnessed a continuation of the trend toward an emphasis on invention, arrangement, and delivery. Style has not been a primary concern.

9. Regrettably, too few evangelistic preachers in the history of preaching were known for their solid exposition of biblical truth and the application of that truth to the lives of their listeners.

# III

## Selecting Material for Evangelistic Preaching

IF A PREACHER ASPIRES to the work of an evangelist, he must be adept at gathering proper and effective material that is biblically based and will move his audience. Much criticism of contemporary evangelists is based on the fact that their sermons have little or no content and are too often full of anecdotes that play on people's emotions. Evangelists frequently fail to honor the apostolic maxim, "Gird up the loins of your mind" (1 Pet. 1:13). They seem to put into their addresses anything and everything other than vital thought. There seems to be a strange mixture of material, including outworn phrases, texts torn from their settings, scraps of autobiography, stories of dubious origin, and sentimental experiences that seem designed to excite feelings and produce immediate impression. Evangelists should, on the other hand, become mental athletes if they are to do justice to the body of revealed truth that they are commissioned to share. The great doctrines of salvation should not be delivered in a slovenly fashion. Poorly constructed and ill-considered sermons are an insult to the majestic gospel of Christ. It was Charles Spurgeon who once said, "High royal truths should ride in a chariot of gold."

At the very outset, three terms must be defined that are regretably often misunderstood, used interchangeably, and taken for granted by many of the authors whose books were surveyed for this chapter. The three terms are *text, subject,* and *theme*. Throughout this book, when the word *text* is used, it refers to the particular preaching portion from the Bible upon which the evangelistic sermon is based. A preaching portion, or passage must possess logical unity and be a complete unit of thought with one central idea. The preaching portion may be one or two paragraphs of Scripture or, on the other hand, a single verse that is spiritually significant and evangelistically appropriate.

When the word *subject* is employed, it refers to neither the text nor the theme, but rather to the central thrust, the one main idea contained in the preaching portion, or text. The subject is the summarizing core of the preaching portion. Furthermore, the subject should be broad enough so that a number of themes can be selected from it.

The *theme* as here used is that particular aspect of the subject that limits it, clarifies it, and amplifies it by suggesting homiletic thoughts worthy of incorporation into an evangelistic sermon. The theme of a sermon will be the particular aspect of the subject just discovered that is to be developed within the particular message. The important thing to remember with reference to the theme is that it grows out of the subject, which, in turn, has been drawn out of the preaching portion. For example, an excellent evangelistic preaching text would be Ephesians 2:1-10; the subject of this preaching portion would be *salvation;* and the theme would be *the necessity of salvation for spiritual life.* The evangelistic preacher must conscientiously seek to be an exegete rather than an eisegete; that is, he must make sure that his subject and theme have been read out of the preaching portion rather than read into it.

## A. The Evangelistic Text

The biblical text must be the foundation of every evangelistic sermon. The evangelist must specialize in the publication of the message of the gospel. He may not have a great number of sermons in readiness, but those that he has must be designed to drive home the content of the gospel as a message of new life to the souls of men. The incarnation, crucifixion, and resurrection of Jesus Christ must make up the hard core of the evangelistic message. There will be no marked advance in evangelistic work apart from an emphatic preaching of Christ crucified, risen, and coming again. Blackwood, in his *Evangelism in the Home Church*, quoted famed evangelist Spurgeon as saying, "Often it is the text, not the sermon, that saves the sinner." J. Wilbur Chapman told of a close friend who felt led to change his sermon text at the last minute. He failed to understand why he had been so led until the next morning when he went through his mail. A letter had come to him that read:

> I was on my way to end my life. I heard the music in your church. Curiosity prompted me to enter. I do not remember anything you said in the sermon, but your text was my mother's text, and as you preached I saw her face and heard her voice. Before you finished your sermon I had accepted my mother's Saviour, and I am writing to thank you for the text you used.[1]

We do not mean to imply that the evangelist ought to preach without extensive preparation, but rather we point to the power of the sacred Word. An evangelistic preaching portion ought to confront the sinner with his lostness, his need of salvation, and the way whereby he can become a "new creation" in Christ Jesus.

In the lecture, the subject dominates everything. In the sermon, the man speaking is so central that in a certain sense the sermon is the man. The sermon is truth passing through the life of the preacher. The preacher's life interprets and enforces that truth. Therefore, the biblical text must grip the preacher and stir his heart before he can hope to stir the imagination and prod the conscience of the hearer.

1. J. Wilbur Chapman, *The Problem of the Work,* pp. 93-94.

The entire Bible, Old and New Testament alike, is a storehouse of source material for the evangelistic preacher. One of the finest books on evangelistic preaching written from a homiletic perspective is the one by Dr. Faris D. Whitesell, professor emeritus at Northern Baptist Theological Seminary, entitled *Evangelistic Preaching and the Old Testament.* That helpful book is filled with relevant ideas for the evangelist who is concerned with finding meaningful and biblical material.[2] Dr. Whitesell gave sixteen reasons why evangelistic preachers should use the Old Testament more often:

1. The Old Testament is the Word of God as much as the New Testament. . . .
2. The Old Testament is glowingly interesting if properly interpreted and applied. . . .
3. Jesus and the apostles set the pattern for using the Old Testament in preaching and teaching. . . .
4. Most of the noted preachers of the past have made large use of the Old Testament. . . .
5. The most successful evangelistic preachers of the present day frequently use the Old Testament source materials. . . .
6. The New Testament can be understood and properly interpreted only against the background of the Old Testament. . . .
7. The evangelistic emphasis should have variety and color in order to maintain interest and produce effect. . . .
8. The Old Testament is a human-interest book. It deals with actual characters and factual history. . . .
9. All New Testament truth is rooted in the Old Testament. . . .

2. G. B. F. Hallock listed five hundred evangelistic texts and subjects in *The Evangelistic Cyclopedia,* pp. 13-24; John W. Etter gave thirteen texts worthy of consideration in *The Preacher and His Sermon,* p. 239; Harry M. North has an excellent chapter on "Evangelistic Subjects and Texts" in his book *Harvest and Reapers,* pp. 175-90; and Faris D. Whitesell, in *Basic New Testament Evangelism,* pp. 185-89, made an outstanding compilation of New Testament evangelistic data relative to effective preaching.
See also Appendix C for eleven sermon starters on various evangelistic texts, subjects, and themes.

10. The Old Testament gives perfect illustrations of New Testament truths. . . .
11. People should be taught the harmony and consistency of the Old Testament with the New. . . .
12. The Old Testament has been and is being vindicated as to accuracy and dependability. . . .
13. An abundance of helps on the Old Testament exists and is available to the average Bible student. . . .
14. The Old Testament is a much larger book than the New Testament, and contains a wider variety of literature. . . .
15. If a pastor or church hopes to reach the Jews in the community for Christ, then it is better to use the Old Testament. . . .
16. The Old Testament is evangelistic. It is full of flaming evangelistic material.[3]

The kind of text selected by the evangelist must not be overlooked or taken lightly. Charles G. Finney emphatically pointed out that a doctrinal text is the best kind of evangelistic text. Said Finney:

> What can a man preach, who preaches no doctrine? If he preaches no doctrine, he preaches no gospel. And if he does not preach it in a practical way, he does not preach the gospel. All preaching should be doctrinal, and all preaching should be practical. The very design of doctrine is to regulate practice. A loose, exhorting style of preaching, may affect the passions, and may produce excitement, but will never sufficiently instruct the people to secure sound conversions.[4]

An evangelistic sermon may be based upon a text in which there is a command to obey or a claim to heed. It may be based on a promise to claim or an incentive to follow. The text may be a solemn admonition or a warning to heed. Whatever the text is, the evangelist ought to seek to catch its true

3. Faris D. Whitesell, *Evangelistic Preaching and the Old Testament,* pp. 13-22.
4. Charles G. Finney, *Lectures on Revivals of Religions,* p. 184.

significance and drive that significance home to his audience.

We should build persuasion right into our evangelism. Without persuasion, without intending for people to become disciples of Jesus Christ, our so-called evangelism is a thin, anemic substitute for the real thing. Persuasion is an essential part of effective evangelism. Lovingly persuading people is essential to effective evangelism and should be a vital part of our Christian expression. There is profit, E. D. Jarvis declared, in preaching from two contrasting texts. For example:

"There was no room for them in the inn" and set over against that: "In my Father's house are many mansions." There you have portrayed, on the one hand, man's inhospitality to God, the refusal to give Him any place, however small, in our intimate lives, and, on the other, the great hospitality of God experienced daily, and expressed here by Jesus, who speaks of the home prepared for us when our life on earth is done.[5]

One of the primary concerns of every evangelist should be his desire not to abuse his preaching portion. Abuse can come through using "stock texts" repeatedly or by reading into the preaching text one's own ideas. With reference to the former, North said:

The bane of much evangelistic preaching has been its sameness and apparentness. The sermons coming from just a few stock texts run in the same grooves of doctrinal expression so that the hearers may anticipate what is coming, being able to guess what quotations and incidents will be used. Can anything else be worse than staleness and dullness on the part of a preacher while he presents the greatest subject ever considered by man?[6]

The textual abuse of eisegesis is deplored by almost every writer in the field of homiletic or evangelistic theory. Probably one of the earliest books written or compiled on evangel-

5. E. D. Jarvis, *If Any Man Minister*, pp. 20-21.
6. North, p. 175.

60

istic preaching is the one edited by Doe, *Eminent Authors on Effective Revival Preaching.* In one of the articles written by T. L. Cuyler, entitled "The Successful Minister," the following advice was given:

> Always get your text first, and plant it, and let it grow up into your sermon; and let the main idea of your text be the trunk-thought of your sermon. Out of this central trunk let the limbs expand, and on its branches let the "fruits of the Spirit" grow. Never commit the absurd folly of building a sermon, and then perching a text on top of it. Never attempt either to cheat your people into the belief that they are hearing a new sermon by swapping off an old text for a new one for the decapitation of its text ought to be as *sure death* to a good discourse as would be the stroke of your own head from your body. The sap of the text should reach the farthest twig of the sermon.[7]

R. A. Torrey expressed the same sentiments years later: "Never write a sermon and then hunt up a text for it. That is one of the most wretched and outrageous things that a man who believes that the Bible is the Word of God can do. It is simply using the Word of God as a label or endorsement for your idea."[8]

According to Johnson in *The Ideal Ministry,* "There will be a clear reason for taking one text rather than another, and for treating that text in one way rather than another, and the reason will be in the soul sought."[9] Other marks of proper treatment of the biblical text may be the persuasiveness, appropriateness, and pointedness of the sermon derived from the text.

The evangelistic preacher must be concerned with properly interpreting any biblical text. He must find the central meaning of the preaching portion. As an evangelist, he needs to

---

7. T. L. Cuyler, "The Successful Minister," in *Eminent Authors on Effective Revival Preaching,* ed. Walter P. Doe, p. 124.
8. Reuben A. Torrey, *How to Work for Christ,* pp. 331-32.
9. Herrick Johnson, *The Ideal Ministry,* p. 486.

have a clear idea in his own mind of exactly what the message of the gospel is. This idea need not be highly elaborate theologically; it may be a simple answer to the question, "What was the distinct message of Jesus to humanity, and what does this mean to the persons to whom the address is to be given?" The evangelistic preacher must remember the interpretive principle that Scripture interprets Scripture, and he should seek to interpret the text honestly and relevantly in light of its context. The evangelist should preach the Bible, not about the Bible. The difference is interpretation and the honest grappling with the preaching portion.

Sumner related a personal experience:

> When just starting out in the ministry, I was impressed on one occasion with the repeated statement in Isaiah, "His hand is stretched out still." I promptly began preparing a message on the love of God, showing how God's hand of mercy is continually stretched out to sinners in spite of repeated rejections. However, I had not gone far before I discovered that the expression, "His hand is stretched out still," refers not to love and mercy, but to wrath and judgment! Immediately I scrapped my sermon plans since there are more than enough passages which do teach God's love for sinners in spite of repeated rejections without twisting verses to suit my fancy.[10]

Pearce listed some interpretive questions having relevance to Christ's death in his chapter on evangelistic preaching:

> What was the purpose, the intent, and the end of Christ's crucifixion?
> The resurrection?
> What does it mean?
> How does it relate to me?
> Does it mean the death of sin and the death of death?
> Does it mean that good is more powerful than evil and that God will have the last word?

10. Robert L. Sumner, *Evangelism: The Church On Fire*, p. 166.

How?

Why?

In what way?

Does it mean that life is significant and meaningful?[11]

The choice of any text is a tremendous responsibility in itself. The Bible is so full of truth, and only a limited amount of time is given to the evangelist to plumb its depths of meaning. Hence, selection of preaching texts becomes a crucial decision on the part of the preacher. Various authors have given helpful suggestions relative to the selection of any evangelistic text. William W. Ayer suggested four rules: (1) choose a text that has evangelistic appeal, and avoid passages of doubtful meaning; (2) avoid choosing a complex passage where the basic meaning is difficult to understand; (3) a study of the Old Testament prophets who gave their messages shortly before the divine judgment fell would be profitable; and (4) a study of the conversion experiences in Acts and the life of Christ would prove beneficial in selecting an appropriate evangelistic text.[12] Riley advised the evangelist to select a text that has an evangelistic objective, that lends itself to elucidation, and that contains elements of encouragement.[13] Coffin observed that an evangelist should choose a text that grips his audience the moment he reads it in the pulpit, that indicates to the audience that he is aware of their needs, that shakes those who are indifferent with the realization that the Christian life is a daring adventure, and that gets under the skin of the complacent who rationalize that they can get along without God. In summary, "One needs texts from which people cannot run away."[14] Torrey exhorted the young evangelist to spend time on his knees in meditation, asking God to give him a text from which to preach; to keep a book of texts in which to jot down his thoughts; to expound a book from

11. J. Winston Pearce, *Planning Your Preachings*, p. 132.
12. William W. Ayer, *Flame for the Altar*, pp. 160-63.
13. W. B. Riley, *The Preacher and His Preaching*, p. 87.
14. Henry Sloane Coffin, *What to Preach*, p. 178.

beginning to end; and to read the Bible until he comes to a text that grips him.[15]

## B. The Evangelistic Subject

A number of the writers on the history of preaching, when speaking of the core idea of a preaching portion, refer to that as the theme rather than the subject. According to the definition used in this book, the theme is a particular aspect of the subject that defines, clarifies, and limits the subject. On the other hand, the subject is the broad central thrust of the preaching portion. In brief, the preaching portion is the foundation of the sermon. The subject must come from that foundation; and the theme is part of the further development of that textually grounded subject.

There are at least four basic characteristics of effective evangelistic subjects. First, the subjects must be concise; that is, they must be "particularized, sharpened, freshened and made clear in some three to six words."[16] Second, they should be timeless truths, having unquestioned relevance for all time. Third, they should be varied. A preacher should not limit himself to those subjects on which he himself thrives. An effective evangelist preaches not only on the subject of God's love and mercy, but also on the subject of God's wrath and judgment. To preach only hobbyhorse subjects is to do a great disservice to the biblical text and to the hearers. Finally, evangelistic subjects should be scriptural; that is, they should be drawn from the particular biblical texts under consideration. A scriptural subject, coupled with the convicting power of the Holy Spirit, is the means whereby a person may be called to repentance and faith in Christ.

The evangelist will find the following subjects to be evangelistically productive:

15. Torrey, pp. 330-31.
16. Faris D. Whitesell, *Evangelistic Preaching and the Old Testament*, p. 42.

Armageddon
Atonement

Broken spirit
Brotherly love

Calvary
Charity
Christ as judge
Christian character
Christian ethics
Christian stewardship
Church
Concern of God
Consecration
Conversion
Cross
Crucifixion of Christ

Death
Deity of Christ
Discipleship

Eternity

Faith
Faithfulness of Christ
Fellowship
Forgiveness
Fundamental Christian beliefs

Gospel
Grace
Guilt

Heaven
Hell
Holiness
Holiness of God

Holy Spirit
Hope
Humanity of Christ

Immortality
Incarnation of Christ
Intercession

Jesus Christ
Judgment
Justification

Kingdom of God

Last days
Law
Lordship
Love of God
Loyalty

Man
Mercy of God
Miracles of Jesus

New heavens and new earth

Obedience

Parables of Jesus
Pardon
Peace
Personal dedication
Personal evangelism
Personal work
Power of Christ
Prayer
Precious promises
Procrastination

Rededication

| | |
|---|---|
| Redemption | Sin |
| Reform | Soul |
| Regeneration | Sovereignty |
| Repentance | Substitution |
| Resurrection | |
| | Temptation |
| Salvation | Truth |
| Sanctification | |
| Second coming | Witnessing |
| Separation | Worldliness |

The selection of the subject must come naturally from the text itself. However, the circumstances in which the evangelist finds himself and the audience to whom he addresses himself will affect the preaching portion from which an appropriate subject is taken. At times an evangelist would do well to select a text and a subject that bring edification and encouragement to the people of God. At other times, the evangelist should select a subject that shakes the lethargic or rebukes cold church members whose inconsistencies are hindering revival. If evangelism rather than revival is the purpose and the audience is mainly composed of the unregenerate, the evangelist would be wise to select a subject that sounds forth God's love and mercy or God's wrath and judgment. Adaptation is the key word when it comes to the proper selection of the subject for an evangelistic occasion.

With reference to the treatment of the subject, the words of Etter are noteworthy:

> If too much stress is laid on one subject, or class of subjects, the convert's character will not be evenly balanced or perfect. Let the preacher guard against using "hobbies" in a revival. Some subjects are more important than others, but all must be treated in proportion to their importance, and with reference to the circumstances of the people. Often, during the progress of a revival, the recurrence of similar circumstances will require that a former sermon be repeated, but with a change of form and language, and also, if possible,

with improvement. Not only should the preacher sometimes repeat sermons, but repeat in the same sermon whatever he sees is not perfectly understood by his hearers.[17]

John A. Broadus, in his classic homiletic work *On the Preparation and Delivery of Sermons,* gave some valuable advice regarding the sequence of subjects to be considered by the evangelist:

> A general sequence like the following is often found useful: First address the church, seeking to arouse a more active spiritual life, to recall the worldly and quicken the pious, awakening in all the spirit of prayer and of intense concern for the salvation of others; then present for several meetings the terrors of the law, searching the conscience, arousing concern for sin, the fear of judgment, and the consequent imperative need of a Saviour; then set forth the mercy and love of God as displayed in the gospel of his Son, the certainty and completeness of the divine forgiveness of sin upon repentance and faith; and finally urge immediate decision and acceptance of the gospel terms, with public confession of Christ. Whatever order may be observed, none of these topics can be safely omitted from a series of revival sermons.[18]

Although the evangelist can combine several of these subjects into one sermon for the sake of time, he must guard against the temptation of overemphasizing any one area in the subject sequence. For example, some evangelists in their zeal for an immediate decision neglect to deal with those subject areas that naturally and logically precede personal confession of faith in Christ. The unhappy result in such cases is that people are induced to make a public commitment to Christ quite apart from any inward conviction of sin and without having sensed their utter need of the Savior.

## C. The Evangelistic Theme

The evangelistic theme is that which is derived from the

17. Etter, pp. 246-47.
18. John A. Broadus, *On the Preparation and Delivery of Sermons,* p. 308.

evangelistic subject. It is not the subject but a particular aspect of the subject that clarifies it, limits it, or defines it. According to Etter, the love of Jesus is the greatest of all gospel themes. Many of the influential evangelistic preachers of the past were known to have emphasized particular themes. Dwight L. Moody stressed the love of God. The human ability and responsibility to respond to the gospel was an earmark of Charles G. Finney. Billy Sunday's favorite theme was the folly of sin and worldliness. In contrast to Sunday was Gypsy Smith, who preached on the beauty of Jesus.

The apparent confusion over subject and theme has already been mentioned. An example of this is the statement by Abbey: "The real power of pulpit evangelism . . . rests on a doctrinal substructure. Sin, grace, atonement, forgiveness, regeneration; these are the potent themes of the evangelist."[19] As can be seen readily, these are not aspects of anything, but merely the broad, centralized core areas of any given preaching portion. The unfortunate confusion of terms may be one of the reasons evangelistic preaching has often been more topical than expository.

Two writers gave helpful advice regarding the characterization of an evangelistic theme. Brastow, in his book *The Work of the Preacher,* noted that an evangelistic theme (in the sense in which this book defines it) is simple, direct, definite, clear, and brief. Such a theme will promote forcefulness and impressiveness with reference to the major thrust of the sermon. Andrew Blackwood pointed out that the theme should also be doctrinal. That will happen automatically if the theme is derived from a subject drawn from the biblical text. A doctrinal theme is the best kind for an evangelist, because creed must always come before conduct. "In the past every evangelistic movement blessed of God has come largely through preaching doctrine. Evangelism has flourished, or languished according to the amount and the fervor of such pulpit work."[20] More-

19. Merrill R. Abbey, *Living Doctrine in a Vital Pulpit,* p. 30.
20. Andrew W. Blackwood, *Doctrinal Preaching for Today,* p. 51.

over, by having some doctrinal emphasis as his evangelistic theme, the preacher avoids such common evangelistic errors as emotionalism, traditionalism (stock phrases), professionalism, vagueness, shallowness, anecdotage (defined by Blackwood as "sickly stories, improbable, impossible, unthinkable"), monotony, unpreparedness, and prayerlessness.

The selection of an appropriate evangelistic theme takes diligence and concentration on the preacher's part, with reference both to his preaching portion and to the needs of the people to whom he is ministering. Themes must be selected that grow out of the main subject matter of the preaching portion. They should be worded so that they present a timeless principle or truth. Evangelistic themes should be selected that "force hearers to heed the gospel message," said Pearce, and "that launch out into the deeps of God and do not always hug the shallows of emotion alone."[21] An evangelist also would do well to select a moving theme. It is always better to have the Word of God move the hearer to a decision for Christ rather than the words of the preacher, which are neither timeless nor infallible.

The results of selecting a theme from a broad subject are fourfold:

> The hearts of the saints will be refreshed .
> A new interest in the people outside the Kingdom will be created and personal work prompted.
> Spiritual power will be generated.
> An atmosphere will be created which will be conducive to the success of the entire evangelistic effort.[22]

Many writers speak about preaching on the "big themes" or "great themes of the gospel." However, they really mean the "big subjects" and "great subjects" of the gospel, according to the definitions used here.

Only one book in the field of either evangelistic or homi-

21. Pearce, p. 134.
22. Roy H. Short, *Evangelistic Preaching*, p. 77.

letic theory gives examples of themes for evangelistic preaching that are aspects of a subject and that clarify, limit, or define the subject, making it more meaningful to the listener. That unique volume is entitled *Evangelistic Preaching* and was written by Roy H. Short. If the preacher's subject were sin, said Short, the following could be possible themes: "the sins of the flesh," "secret sin," "sins of omission," or the "results of sin." If his subject were God, the particular aspects of that subject would be (depending on the particular preaching portion): the "holiness of God," "righteousness of God," "love of God," "judgment of God," or the "grace of God." Short went on to suggest some possible evangelistic themes that answer difficulties people have regarding salvation; some of those difficulties are:

Unwillingness to abandon some pet sin

The presence of intellectual doubts

The fear of not being able to continue once one has taken a stand as a Christian

The tendency to put off to another time the matter of a decision

The impression that becoming a Christian is a matter of feeling rather than a matter of faith

The assumption that the costs of discipleship are too expensive

The fear that one is too great a sinner

Short went on to name the following themes with reference to the subject of the Christian life. First, concerning its demands:

The demand to live a holy life and keep oneself unspotted from the world

The demand to make amends as far as possible for the wrongs which one has done

The demand to practice Christian stewardship of life, and time, and property, and talents

The demand to help build the Kingdom of God in the world

70

Second, concerning its privileges:

> The witness of the Spirit in the heart of the believer
> The joy of companionship with the Eternal
> The richness of fellowship with God's people
> The sheer delight of living a life of service and Christian helpfulness
> Having a share in bringing in the glorious day when the kingdoms of this world shall become the Kingdom of our Lord and of His Christ

Finally, Short suggested three themes with reference to the church:

> The obligation of identity with the church by baptism
> The duty and privilege of church attendance in the interest of nurturing the spiritual life
> The obligation of loyal support of the institution of which Christ is the Head, and for whose life He died[23]

The title of an evangelistic sermon should grow out of the theme. It should not be merely the theme itself set off in quotation marks, but rather such a rewording of the theme as will attract attention and create interest. A title is of questionable value unless it conveys at least a hint about the nature of the message to follow. An evangelistic sermon title should not be more than four or five words long. It should be characterized by imaginativeness, creativity, and anticipatory power. Furthermore, it ought to have advertising appeal that catches the unsuspecting off guard.

The following evangelistic sermon titles were suggested by Pearce:

> "From Rags to Riches"
> "On Looking for a Kingdom"
> "Know Your Heart's Condition"
> "The Most Unforgettable Person I Know"
> "Soul Erosion"

23. Ibid., pp. 75-76.

71

"The Best Things Are Not Free"
"Songs in the Night"
"How to Become a Christian"
"What Christ Does For Men"
"How to Take God's Help"
"How to Trust God's Care"
"What Is Right With the Church"
"This Life Is Worth Living"
"God and Man's Need"
"Begin Living Today"
"Why Not Try Christ's Way?"
"The Recoil of Repudiated Responsibilities"
"Facing Failure With Faith"
"When Life Tumbles In, What Then?"
"The Comfort and Challenge of Christianity"
"A Good Word for Jesus Christ"
"All This, and Heaven, Too"
"A Magnificent Obsession"
"When the Roll Is Called Down Here"
"We Sail Under Sealed Orders"
"On Going Back to Go Forward"
"What Are You Standing For?"
"What in the World Are You Doing for Heaven's Sake?"
"The Kind of Repentance That Does Some Good"
"Our God Is Able"
"The Naturalness of Faith"
"Impossible to Escape God"
"Learn to Be Alone Together"
"The Satisfaction of Living Your Life With God"
"Magnificent Reminders"[24]

Weldon Crossland, in his book *How to Increase Church Membership and Attendance,* gave some additional effective evangelistic sermon titles:

"Every Man's Life a Plan of God"
"Three Steps to God"
"What Jesus Means to Me"

24. Pearce, p. 136.

"Do We Really Want God?"
"The Secret of Victorious Living"
"Christ Has All the Answers"
"You Belong to God"
"This Life Is Worth Living"
"Beyond the Old Frontiers"
"If Christ Had Not Come"
"What Is God Doing Now?"
"The Church and the World"
"For Christ and His Church"
"Eventually, Why Not Now?"
"The Power to See It Through"
"The Ultimate Question"
"What Think Ye of Christ?"
"In Partnership With God"
"Life and How to Build It"[25]

## D. The Classification of an Evangelistic Sermon

Edgar W. Work classified evangelistic sermonic methodology according to kind. His is the only work we know of in either evangelistic or homiletic theory that makes such a classification. Work's book would fall into the category of evangelistic theory. He suggested the following five kinds of sermonic methodology: (1) the illustrative, narrative kind that is characterized by exhortation (rather than exposition) ; (2) the didactic form of evangelism that is mainly concerned with factual content; (3) the personal type which appeals to present realities and needs of life; (4) the scriptural kind, where the evangelistic truth leaps forth from the biblical text itself; and (5) the doctrinal type in which Christian truth is explained and enforced scripturally.[26]

From the present writers' perspective, kinds four and five are the ideal sermonic methods as far as evangelistic preaching is concerned. The biblical text is the only safe foundation for

25. Weldon Crossland, *How to Increase Church Membership and Attendance*, pp. 35-36.
26. Edgar W. Work, *Every Minister His Own Evangelist*, pp. 39-40.

calling men to a changed life-style. The widely accepted belief that evangelistic preaching should be only topical and emotional does not harmonize with Work's idea of evangelistic preaching. His comment is noteworthy:

> Many a minister would find if he tried that his own way of preaching can be made evangelistic. Does he preach historical sermons? He can do it in such a way as to move the soul in the direction of God. Is he a doctrinal preacher? He can so preach doctrine as to clarify the issues of life, especially the main issue of sin. Is he biographical, literary, scientific, hortatory? He can put a spiritual appeal into each of these forms. Does he handle skillfully science, current events, ethics, patriotism? There is always an opportunity to preach Christ.[27]

All preaching, whether didactic, apologetic, hortatory, or expository, should be permeated with the spirit of evangelism. The ultimate objective should be to bring men to Christ in salvation and service and to train them for soul-winning and service.

## E. The Functional Elements of an Evangelistic Sermon

The functional elements of an evangelistic sermon are the persuasive elements of the sermon—namely, the explanation, argumentation, illustration, and application—which support the main structural elements of the sermon, such as the introduction, discussion (main sermon body), and conclusion.

### 1. APPLICATION

The application of an evangelistic sermon is of vital importance. The work edited by Doe includes a section by John A. Broadus on application. Broadus's definition of an application is significant: "The application in a sermon is not merely an appendage to the discussion, or a subordinate part

27. Ibid., p. 40.

of it, but is the main thing to be done. Spurgeon says: 'Where the application begins, there the sermon begins.' "[28] In an evangelistic sermon, the application is one of the areas most needing development.

The application of an evangelistic sermon must be directed toward the lives of people. The pastor's program of evangelism should have three emphases. Those emphases should include person to person soul-winning, revivals, and a constructive teaching ministry. A church, from pulpit to primary department, should be burdened to see people coming to Christ for salvation. A church that works passionately to see people continually coming to Christ is evangelistic.

The application cannot afford to be remote. It must have something to do with all the events of the most commonplace day of the humblest man.

Persuasiveness is also characteristic of an effective evangelistic application.

At this point the sermon must be distinguished from an essay—it must motivate the hearers to positive action. The evangelistic preacher should be all the time pleading for a verdict. The entire content of the message should be such that the listeners will understand the truth more clearly and be persuaded to accept it. The test of a good sermon is what happens to the man in the pew.

Furthermore, an appropriate application is definitely related to the content of the preaching portion.

The application must be separated from the interpretation. Interpretation deals with the question, What does the text mean in its context? Application, on the other hand, deals with the question, What does the text mean to me? The application must follow an interpretation that has captured the biblical writer's original intent when he was inspired by the Holy Spirit.

A fourth key to the application is that it must be personal.

28. John A. Broadus, "Application," in Doe, p. 218.

The hearer should be able to respond in his heart, "This is for me." The application must awaken within the hearer a desire to carry out the content of the message in his particular context of living. Porter summarized well:

> Preaching should have a direct application to the hearers. They must be made to understand that the preacher means them—is preaching to them, and about them. This is indispensible. Nothing will be done without it. While the people suppose their minister is talking about the Jews, or the Sodomites, or any other than themselves, he preaches in vain. They must be made to feel that they are aimed at, involved; that the object of the preacher is to save them. A distinguished minister has well said, "A sermon without an application is like a body without a soul."[29]

The implementation of an evangelistic application rests in the hands of the sermonizer. He cannot assume that his job is merely to give the meaning of the text and then have the audience make its own application. To effectively apply his evangelistic message, the evangelist must be cognizant of the trends, currents, and tendencies of his day. He must seek to be knowledgeable in the contemporary issues of society. He must be an avid reader of secular as well as sacred literature to sharpen his perspective in applying biblical truth. An ability to relive and recount the commonplace, everyday situations of life also helps him to drive home significant spiritual truths. He must seek variety of application to constantly deepen the spiritual insight of his hearers. Moreover, such variety also helps to keep his own mind spiritually and mentally alert. Obvious or monotonous applications can kill the sermon. An evangelist must constantly update and rethink his applications to make them appropriate. Such revision will render his sermon more effective and timely. The evangelist must also seek to balance his application to individuals specifically and to groups collectively. As Muncy stated:

29. James Porter, *Revivals of Religion*, p. 72.

The individual must not be lost in the group and allowed to place the responsibility for his sins upon the group. Even in discussing applied Christianity from the pulpit, the preacher must never lose sight of the fact that everyone must give an account of himself unto God.[30]

## 2. ARGUMENTATION

In the field of classical rhetoric, argumentation has to do with providing rational proof to establish or justify a particular statement. According to Quintilian, "An argument is a process of reasoning affording a proof, by which one thing is gathered from another, and which establishes what is doubtful by reference to what is certain."[31]

It is at the point of argumentation that evangelistic preaching receives its greatest criticism, even from those who are its proponents. Roy Short in *Evangelistic Preaching* stated:

> Evangelistic preaching today needs to be redeemed. It needs to be redeemed from identification with the mouthing of platitudes and the attempted defense of indefensible ideas. Too much of what has passed for evangelistic preaching has been intellectually weak, and frequently untenable ideas have been uttered with such vehemence and dogmatism as to provoke thinking people to disgust. It needs to be redeemed from pious insincerity, and from false tears and pulpit tones, and weak and pitiful attempts at dramatic effects. It needs to be redeemed from trickery in handling people and from the prostitution of so holy a thing as the Gospel to unworthy ends. Only an evangelism of Christian quality can commend itself to a generation with a high quotient of intelligence.[32]

The need for careful argumentation cannot be overemphasized, and no earnest evangelist should ever rule out ar-

30. W. L. Muncy, *New Testament Evangelism for Today*, p. 198.
31. Lester Thonssen, ed., *Selected Readings in Rhetoric and Public Speaking*, p. 119.
32. Short, p. 18.

gument from the pulpit. Riley, in his book *The Preacher and His Preaching,* showed that the earthly ministry of our Lord and the historical record of the book of Acts were saturated with argument. Moreover, the evangelists who have been greatly used of God were men who logically developed the great doctrines of the faith, namely, the authority of Scripture, the deity of Christ, the atonement, the reality of the resurrection, the credibility of the ascension, and the assurance of the second advent. Charles Spurgeon and Reuben Torrey used logical argument to prove to their audiences the validity of the claims of Christ. Their intellectual defense of Christ's claims was greatly used by God in the conversion of many people to Christ.

The evangelistic sermon must be logical in its argument. The sermonizer must take great care to present his message in such a way that his hearers can follow the logic he has built upon the text he is expounding. To be logical, the preacher must delve deeply into the context and content of his preaching portion. He must not be content merely to hit the high spots but must discipline himself to become thoroughly knowledgeable on the particular passage from which he is preaching.

The evangelistic sermon must be convincing in its argument. To this end, the preacher must direct his comments to the whole man, challenging both his mind and his emotions. The fuel of content must be balanced with the fire of emotion. Too often evangelists have more fire than fuel. A convincing argument derived from the Scriptures themselves will assure the sermonizer of his desired results.

Reasonableness is a third characteristic of argumentation from an evangelistic viewpoint. The affirmations the evangelist makes should satisfy the mind as well as prompt the heart to action. Reasonable argument can result only from a careful and lucid exposition of the Scriptures. Similarly, the application that follows the exposition should be rational, coordinated, and coherent. The effective evangelist will become a master at reasonably uniting creed and conduct.

Finally, the argumentation of an evangelistic sermon should be positive. The sermon should focus on those affirmations of the Word that lift one out of himself and bring him into a personal confrontation with Jesus Christ. If the text is negative and full of warning, the evangelist should be true to the text. However, his conclusion should present the positive side of the negatives he has expounded. To be positive, the sermon must stay away from indefiniteness and vague generalities.

Argumentation is mainly concerned with proof. Robert L. Sumner's book *Evangelism: The Church On Fire* is helpful at this point. "Power in the pulpit," Sumner said, "will be determined by the degree in which you offer proof for your contentions." In a later paragraph he added, "No man has a right to enter the pulpit unless he understands what constitutes proof and agrees to present that proof to his hearers."[33] However, what Sumner said is only partially true; it should be noted that the moral character of the preacher and the supernatural promptings of the Spirit of God are also invaluable aids in building an effective argument.

Two kinds of proof are set forth by Sumner relative to evangelistic sermonic methodology. The primary source of proof for the evangelist is the revelation of the Word of God. "If the Bible does not teach it, he has no business preaching it. The power of proof must be grounded in the Word of God."[34] The secondary source of proof is the realm of human experience. "Many a message has contained ample strong meat for the hearers, only to go over the heads and miss the hearts simply because it lacked the illumination of illustration."[35]

33. Sumner, pp. 137-38.
34. Ibid., p. 138.
35. Ibid., pp. 143-44.

In summary, the evangelist who builds effective argumentation into his sermon will preach truth that is logical, convincing, reasonable, positive, and biblically authoritative.

### 3. ILLUSTRATION

The functional element receiving the most attention from the writers in the field of homiletic and evangelistic theory is the illustration. Whole books have been published that categorize evangelistic sermonic illustrations.[36]

Etymologically, the word *illustration* comes from the word *in* and the Latin word *lustro,* meaning "to shine." Simply put, illustration means "to shine in." An illustration takes an unfamiliar truth and makes the light "shine in" upon it by comparing it to a familiar truth. Ozora Davis, in his work *Evangelistic Preaching,* described illustrations as "windows" that let in the light of the truth of the message. That was also the philosophy of Moody, who once said, "A sermon without illustrations is like a house without windows." Illustrations clarify what is obscure. Illustrations unfold that which is abstruse. They may be used to explain, to prove, or to adorn the biblical text. As Burrell stated, illustrations, regardless of form, "break up a commonplace paragraph like a sunburst or a trumpet blast."[37] In the final analysis, the illustrations used in any given evangelistic sermon will render it successful or unsuccessful. Whitesell advised, "If the illustrations raise doubts as to their veracity, or indicate boastfulness on the part of the preacher, or lack freshness and point, they may do more harm than good."[38]

Evangelistic illustrations are valuable because they attract and hold the attention of the man in the pew. Moreover, they

---

36. Hallock's book contains four hundred fifty evangelistic illustrations (pp. 25-124). Aquilla Webb in *One Thousand Evangelistic Illustrations* categorized illustrations for evangelistic purposes under sixty headings (pp. 15-349).
37. David J. Burrell, *The Sermon: Its Construction and Delivery,* p. 105.
38. Faris D. Whitesell, *Evangelistic Preaching and the Old Testament,* p. 48.

clarify and amplify the truth of the message by fastening the truth in the mind of the listener, who often identifies with it. Illustrations are also important because they throw light on that which is often difficult to understand. A thoughtful and relevant illustration breaks up sermonic monotony. To speak continuously without any illustrations is to cause people to grow weary. Illustrations tend to be remembered long after the preacher has departed, thus becoming a lingering force in the spiritual life of the listener.

Effective evangelistic illustrations are relevant. It is wise to use books of compiled sermonic illustrations sparingly, as they tend to be hard to understand and out of date.

Illustrations must be factual. There is nothing more dishonest than for a speaker to conjure up a hypothetical illustration and then give it as though he had been an eyewitness to a real event. The preacher must adhere to the facts when using illustrations. Exactness is a part of a speaker's concern for facts.

Illustrations should be distinctive. That is, they should not be run-of-the-mill anecdotes, but rather fresh, innovative, and impressive. On the other hand, they ought to emphasize that which people have in common in the everyday experiences of life. Said Finney,

> The object of an illustration is, to make people *see the truth,* not to bolster up pulpit dignity. A minister whose heart is in the work, does not use an illustration to make people stare, but to make them see the truth. . . . The illustration should, if possible, be a matter of common occurrence, and the *more* common the occurrence, the more sure it will be, not to fix attention upon itself, but it serves as a *medium through* which the truth is conveyed.[39]

Variety of illustration is also a characteristic of great evangelistic preaching. To overuse one form of illustration and

39. Finney, p. 194.

exclude other meaningful ones is to render a sermon ineffective. For example, in using only quotations or personal experiences throughout the message, a speaker omits other vital sources of illustrations—such as history, poetry, hymnology, science, and current events—that may better illustrate the point he is trying to make. An evangelistic preacher must not only be adept at using illustrations, but he should employ the best one at the proper time and with the proper force.

There are many sources from which preachers can draw effective illustrations for evangelistic sermons. Probably the best ones are the everyday situations of life—the commonplace occurrences with which people can readily identify. The following sources can provide good illustrations for evangelistic sermons.

| | |
|---|---|
| Anecdotes | Magazines |
| Art | |
| Astronomy | Nature |
| Athletics | Newspapers |
| Biography | Personal experience |
| Books | Poetry |
| | Proverbs |
| Essays | |
| Experiences of others | Quotations |
| Fiction | Religious life |
| History | Science |
| Human life | Scripture |
| Hymnology | Short stories |
| Literature | Visible objects |

The best way to gather illustrations is to be a constant observer of people, places, and things. One must become a careful student of the simple things of life and mix freely with people from all walks of life. Another valuable way to gather illustrations is to be a disciplined reader of both sacred and secular literature. A wise preacher reads with pen in hand to record maxims and thoughts that may fit into his preaching program at a later date. Those reading notes can be kept in a looseleaf binder and serve as a vast storehouse of pertinent illustrative material. Torrey, in *How to Work for Christ,* suggested that illustrative power can be gained by making it a practice to talk with children on a regular basis. He also suggested that a study of the masters of illustration in the history of preaching would prove beneficial to one desiring to increase his illustrative ability.[40]

The way in which the sermonizer uses illustrations is most important:

- Illustrations should be kept close to life.
- Illustrations should be accurate and exact.
- Illustrations should be rejected if they bear any falsehood or exaggeration.
- Deathbed illustrations should be used cautiously, if at all.
- Personal illustrations should be used only occasionally, and then with discretion.
- Illustrations must not turn the attention of the listener from the subject to the illustration itself.
- Do not talk about illustrating; just illustrate.
- Make sure you have something to illustrate before you use illustrations.
- Make certain that your illustrations illustrate.
- Avoid employing threadbare and fictitious stories as illustrations.
- Stay away from the temptation to take a story that someone else told of his friend and say that "a friend of mine" did this or that.

40. The following preachers from chapter 2 are known as good illustrators: Chrysostom, Dominic, Anthony of Padua, John Tauler of Strasburg, John Geiler of Kaisersberg, Hugh Latimer, Paolo Segneri, Rowland Hill, Leigh Richmond, Charles G. Finney, Dwight L. Moody, Samuel P. Jones, and Billy Graham. A study of their sermons would be most helpful to an aspiring evangelist.

- Use illustrations effectively in either the introduction or conclusion of your evangelistic sermon.
- Do not use every illustration that comes to your mind; use only the best.

Illustrations are only windows to let in light. They should not become the major part of any evangelistic sermon. The Bible text must be central. No more than one illustration should be used for a single sermonic idea. It is also true that using illustrations for the sake of illustrations weakens any message. As Edgar Work pointed out:

> Unless the preacher guards himself with rigid care, he will overload such evangelistic sermons with incidents, illustrations, and stories of life. To some extent he may lose the advantage of Scriptural depth, and will tend to run in shallow waters. The actual evangelistic content of such sermons is likely to be small except with men of unusual power. It is the thin edge of the Gospel that they use, rather than its wide and deep measure. They will have atmosphere, and that is often persuasive, but atmosphere too easily evaporates.[41]

## F. Methods of Preparation for an Evangelistic Sermon

There are some basic, general guidelines for the preparation of an evangelistic sermon. First, a consistent prayer life develops a preacher who is dependent upon God. Before one can preach an evangelistic sermon, he must have an evangelistic heart. Second, a systematic study of the Word of God creates a knowedgeable and biblical preacher. Third, a disciplined reading of all available source material (critical and devotional commentaries, journal articles, Christian biographies, popular works, and literary classics) having relevance to one's preaching portion leads to a well-informed preacher. The evangelistic sermon must be intellectually respectable. The

41. Work, p. 38.

evangelistic sermon should be as thought-provoking as any other sermon. It should be the result of hard and careful preparation and much prayer. Finally, daily exchange with people in all walks of life produces a well-balanced preacher.

Faris D. Whitesell, in his book *Evangelistic Preaching and the Old Testament,* gave some very valuable suggestions on the preparation of evangelistic messages on Old Testament characters, types, books, chapters, paragraphs, and word studies. His breakdown was simple and to the point:

### How to Prepare Evangelistic Sermons from Old Testament Characters

1. Decide on the character you wish to use. . . .
2. Read what some good Bible dictionary or encyclopaedia says about your character. . . .
3. Read the Bible references carefully. . . .
4. Look for significant facts readily applicable to your hearers. . . .
5. With this preparation, continue to pray about and brood over your material and write down every suggestion and idea that comes to mind. . . .
6. Now read all the material available on the subject of your message. . . .
7. Arrange this material into a good sermon outline.[42]

### Suggestions for Preparing Evangelistic Messages on Old Testament Types

1. Bring out the primary, original, historical, and local meanings of the passage along with the typical meaning. . . .
2. Do not press the details too far. . . .
3. Keep all typical teaching harmonious with the other teachings of the Bible. . . .
4. Emphasize the New Testament antitype. . . .
5. Observe a proper balance in frequency of typical messages. . . .

42. Faris D. Whitesell, *Evangelistic Preaching and the Old Testament,* pp. 68-70.

6. Consult plenty of references so you will not be led off on a tangent by some one writer's peculiar ideas. . . .
7. Go slowly in claiming to find original discoveries concerning types.[43]

### Pointers on Preparing Bible Book Evangelistic Sermons

1. Start with the simpler, easier books first, such as Ruth or Jonah. . . .
2. Study the book carefully in the English translations, reading and rereading it until its message grips you. . . .
3. Watch for and note great evangelistic emphases, texts and illustrations. . . .
4. Try to discover the main subject of the book, and then the main divisions, and these will make the framework for your sermon. . . .
5. Read the analyses and discussions by other writers on the particular book being studied. . . .
6. Select major evangelistic emphases for your message and omit minor considerations. . . .
7. Relate the whole discussion to current situations. . . .
8. Connect it with the New Testament and put Christ into it.[44]

### How to Prepare Evangelistic Sermons on Old Testament Chapters

1. Choose easy chapters first. . . .
2. Study the chapter first in its relation to the whole book in which it is located. . . .
3. Break the chapter up into its natural and logical divisions. . . .
4. Read the commentaries and Bible helps after you have come to the end of your own ideas on the text.[45]

Whitesell gave this advice on preparing evangelistic sermons on Old Testament paragraphs:

43. Ibid., pp. 89-90.
44. Ibid., pp. 129-30.
45. Ibid., pp. 138-39.

Select the easy paragraphs first. . . . Find out exactly what the paragraph says, then what it means, and finally how to apply it helpfully. Pay close attention to the immediate context and the larger context; study the main words carefully; use all the commentaries and helps you have; make a simple, logical, progressive, positive outline; keep thinking about the passage at least for several days; . . . preach . . . without notes . . . ; and appeal for decisions.[46]

### How to Work Out Word-Study Sermons

1. Equip yourself at least with Young's or Strong's concordance; and, if possible, with lexicons, and other grammatical aids. . . .
2. Select a word, find it in the large concordance, and read the references. . . .
3. Study all forms of a word. . . .
4. Out of the many references studied, note the particular verses and illustrative references you wish to use. . . .
5. Now develop this material into homiletical order and build it up into a complete sermon by the usual sermonic processes.[47]

The local pastor ought to give serious consideration to the development of an evangelistic preaching program. The pulpit still offers him his supreme evangelistic opportunity. There appears to be a correlation between a fresh surging of spiritual life in a church and an increased burden upon the people of God to plead with unbelievers to give their hearts to Christ. A preaching program must always take into consideration the needs of the congregation as well as the preacher's personal development in the areas from which he proposes to preach. A preaching program will enable the preacher to make certain that the whole counsel of God is proclaimed rather than just his favorite hobbyhorses.

Any evangelistic preaching program must have Christ at

46. Ibid., p. 151.
47. Ibid., pp. 178-79.

the center; His character, claims, and work must become the focal points of development. Pearce suggested the following possible evangelistic series that might be worked into a successful preaching program:

The Friends of Jesus
The Enemies of Jesus
Questions Jesus Asked
Questions Asked of Jesus
Questions Asked About Jesus
Names for the Followers of Jesus
Names for the Church

The Parables
The Miracles
Personal Evangelism Cases of Jesus
Conversations of Jesus
The Sermons of Jesus
Crises in the Life of Christ
The Prayers of Jesus[48]

Davis, in his book *Evangelistic Preaching,* outlined a program of evangelistic preaching with thirty-two subjects and texts:

"The Man of Nazareth"—John 19:5
"The Great Teacher"—Luke 21:37-38
"Jesus the Moral Radical"—Mark 7:21
"Christ Claims Us for the Highest Life"—John 1:42
"The Master's Motive Our Master Motive"—Phil. 2:5
"Christ the Object of Love and Faith"—1 Pet. 1:8-9
"The Living Christ Our Constant Comrade"—Gal. 2:20
"Religion Inevitable"—Psalm 27:8
"What Is God Like?"—John 14:9
"Sundering Sin"—Rom. 3:23
"Good News"—2 Cor. 5:19
"Parable of the Soils"—Mark 4:9
"A New Mind"—Rom. 2:4
"Obedience the Test of Love"—Luke 6:46
"Faith That Saves"—Eph. 2:8
"True to the Colors"—Matt. 10:32
"The Christian Ideal of Life"—Phil. 1:9-11
"Growing a Soul"—2 Pet. 3:18

48. Pearce, p. 137.

"The Purpose of Christian Character"—John 17:19
"The Chorus of Christian Character"—2 Pet. 1:5-7
"The House of Man's Soul"—1 Cor. 3:16; 6:19-20
"Temptation and God"—1 Cor. 10:13
"Prevailing Prayer"—James 5:16
"Who Is My Neighbor?"—Luke 10:29-37
"The Living Church"—Eph. 1:22, 23
"Citizens and Athletes of the Gospel"—Phil. 1:27
"The Gospel of the Kingdom"—Matt. 4:23
"Entering the Kingdom"—Matt. 7:21; 18:3
"Laws of the Kingdom"—Matt. 5-7; 22:35-40
"The Privileges of the Kingdom"—Rom. 14:17
"Loyalty to the King"—John 13:13
"Sons of the Resurrection"—Luke 20:36[49]

49. Ozora S. Davis, *Evangelistic Preaching*, pp. 95-195.

# IV

## *Sermonic Structure for Evangelistic Preaching*

THE ORGANIZATION of the material that has been discovered through a careful analysis of the biblical text and context is one of the most neglected areas in evangelistic preaching. Moreover, it is at this point that evangelistic preaching has suffered the most from being separated from the homiletic disciplines. Arrangement in classical rhetoric was one of the tests of a good speech, according to Aristotle.

Of the many books that were surveyed for this study, very few deal with how to arrange an evangelistic message. Many of the writers assumed that if one is called to be an evangelist, he need not worry about homiletic arrangement. Several books gave helpful evangelistic outlines and model sermons without taking the time to explain how they were formulated. Unfortunately, the lack of information on how to arrange an evangelistic sermon has contributed to the many spurious forms of evangelistic preaching receiving widespread acceptance in local church meetings and even on radio and television. If a preacher can "holler" and be "charismatic," he must be gifted as an "evangelist." Any form of intellectual activity (which is required to arrange an evangelistic sermon logically and reasonably) is "unspiritual." Such a philosophy can only hinder rather than help the pulpit evangelist.

### A. THE IMPORTANCE OF EVANGELISTIC SERMONIC ARRANGEMENT

As Roy Short in *Evangelistic Preaching* said:

In no type of preaching is the demand for homiletical skill and conscientious preparation greater, for in no other type of preaching is more involved. The effectiveness of an evangelistic sermon may spell the difference between darkness and light, eternal death and eternal life for some soul.[1]

Logical sermonic arrangement is also imperative if the preacher is to deliver his sermon extemporaneously. More is said of that in the chapter on sermonic presentation. Suffice it to say here that logical arrangement will not only help the listeners remember longer that which is being preached to them, but it will also enable the preacher to recall his points more quickly and accurately during his exposition of the Word. When an evangelist delivers his message extemporaneously without prior thought to sermonic arrangement, his sermon will lack coherence and be full of logical inconsistencies. When that occurs, the preacher overstresses emotion in his message to make up for the lack and to cover up the intellectual blunders he may have committed by neglecting preparatory arrangement. A well-defined train of thought, divided naturally at the point of emphasis in the biblical text, will assure the preacher of a thoughtful, logical, rational, and positive sermon.

Coherent evangelistic sermonic arrangement is based upon the preaching of the apostles. Leighton Ford, in his book *The Christian Persuader,* said that Peter's pentecostal sermon in Acts 2:12-40 had all the marks of a classical evangelistic address. Ford discussed the six components of Peter's sermon:

1. He begins with an explanation (Acts 2:14-21). This takes the form of a personal testimony. . . .
2. Peter continues with a proclamation—asserting the facts of Jesus' career—His mighty works, His death, His resurrection (Acts 2:22-24) . . . .
3. He makes an accusation. "This Jesus . . . you crucified and killed by the hands of lawless men." . . .

1. Roy H. Short, *Evangelistic Preaching,* p. 64.

92

4. He proceeds with a disputation (Acts 2:25-35), showing how the facts of the story of Jesus fit in with the prophecies of the Old Testament. . . .
5. He builds to a declaration, ". . . God has made him both Lord and Christ, this Jesus whom you crucified" (Acts 2:36). . . .
6. He concludes with an invitation to ". . . Repent, and be baptized every one of you in the name of Jesus Christ for the forgiveness of your sins . . ." (Acts 2:38), and an exhortation to "Save yourselves from this crooked generation" (Acts 2:40).[2]

## B. The Evangelistic Sermonic Process

Only three works out of all those surveyed for this study gave any kind of process or steps to follow in constructing an effective evangelistic sermon. R. A. Torrey, in *How to Work for Christ,* gave eight steps the preacher should follow in constructing an evangelistic sermon:

I. Get your text or subject. . . .
II. Find your points. . . .
III. Select your points. . . .
IV. Arrange your points. . . .
V. Plan your introduction. . . .
VI. Illustrate your points. . . .
VII. Arrange your conclusion. . . .
VIII. Think your sermon out closely.[3]

V. L. Stanfield suggested that one should first develop the body of his message, then formulate his introduction, and finally arrange his conclusion.

Faris D. Whitesell listed seven steps in the arrangement of an evangelistic sermon:

1. A subject, title, or topic. . . .
2. The introduction. . . .
3. The proposition, or thesis. . . .

2. Leighton Ford, *The Christian Persuader,* pp. 94-95.
3. Reuben A. Torrey, *How to Work for Christ,* pp. 329-38.

4. The divisions, or points. . . .
5. The discussion. . . .
6. Illustrations. . . .
7. The conclusion.[4]

Although Whitesell's process is logical, it does not give the preacher any explanation about which step is to have priority over the other steps; that is, Whitesell's breakdown gives the finished form an evangelistic sermon ought to take but does not explain how to get that finished form.

In an earlier book one of the present writers gave a basic, eight-step process for the construction of a biblical sermon, a process that is appropriate for anyone who wishes to build an effective evangelistic message. The eight steps are:

    I. Determine the Subject. . . .
   II. Select the Theme. . . .
  III. Formulate a Proposition. . . .
  IV. Establish a Transitional Sentence. . . .
   V. Develop Main Divisions. . . .
  VI. Amplify the Main Divisions. . . .
 VII. Formulate an Introduction. . . .
VIII. Formulate a Conclusion.[5]

To construct a biblical evangelistic sermon, one must start with the preaching portion. From the biblical text a subject must be chosen, from which a relevant theme is derived.

### C. The Proposition of an Evangelistic Sermon

After choosing an appropriate subject and theme, the evangelistic preacher must seek to formulate a proposition. Whitesell's definition of a proposition is helpful: "The proposition is the gist of the sermon, the sermon condensed into one sentence, the spinal column running through the message. It is

4. Faris D. Whitesell, *Evangelistic Preaching and the Old Testament*, pp. 42-49.
5. Lloyd M. Perry, *Biblical Preaching for Today's World*, pp. 44-60. Two supplemental steps after the eight basic steps have been met are the addition of illustrative material and the formulation of an appropriate title.

the thing you wish to prove, and [it] becomes the core of the whole message."[6] Another explanation of the proposition is also helpful:

> The proposition occupies the focal point in the sermon outline. This part of the sermon has been referred to by different homiletical writers as the central idea, the controlling assertion, the statement, the big truth, the subject sentence, and the thesis. It is this sentence which is the integrating center of the sermon. It promotes stability of structure, unity of thought, and forcefulness of impact. It proclaims the truth which the sermonizer desires to establish and apply. The proposition announces the theme in sentence form. It should embody the principal or most striking truth of the scriptural portion on which the man is preaching. It is important that this sentence be true to the impact of Scripture and also that it be relevant to human experience. Great preaching should be in the present tense. It must speak to the concerns of the day and in the thought forms and language of that day. The proposition, in other words, must be stated in the form of a timeless truth which was valid for Bible times and is still valid for the day in which it is being preached. Since it is a timeless truth, no proper names other than that of deity should be included within it.[7]

Propositions can be presented as affirmations or as questions. They may be statements of evaluation or judgment: "Praying is profitable"; of obligation or duty: "It is necessary for Christians to engage in intercessory prayer"; or of activity without stated obligation: "We can become more effective in praying." Whatever the form, they must contain the sermon in a nutshell and be true to the biblical text.

The characteristics of a good proposition are fourfold: (1) it should be general, but not to the extent that it could fit several sermons; (2) it should be specifically drawn from the subject matter of the text, becoming self-evident upon careful

6. Whitesell, *Evangelistic Preaching and the Old Testament*, p. 43.
7. Perry, pp. 47-48.

consideration; (3) it should be relatively brief, capable of being stated in one concise and crisp sentence; and (4) it should be unambiguous. It should not contain any figures of speech, mixed metaphors, or proper names.

In the final analysis, the proposition is the main difference between an organized and a disorganized evangelistic sermon. The sermonizer should not hesitate to spend much time formulating a good proposition. Such time is never wasted and often speeds the compilation of the rest of the sermon. Of Finney it was said, "He carefully and slowly laid down and discussed the fundamental proposition upon which action was to be based, so that whatever movement of feeling there was should be well grounded in a perception of the truth."[8]

## D. The Transitional Process of an Evangelistic Sermon

Following the formulation of a proposition, the sermonizer must establish a transitional sentence. This is the rhetorical bridge between the core of the sermon, the proposition, and the development of the sermon, which is found in the body of the message. The transitional sentence is formulated by applying six questions to the proposition that has just been established, which in turn will guide the evangelist in the fuller development of his sermon. The six questions from which one will be chosen are as follows: (1) How can I? (2) Why should I? (3) When should I? (4) Where should I? (5) Where can I? (6) Why is it? Within these six questions are four interrogative adverbs (how, why, when, and where) that must be related to the proposition.

There are basically three parts to a well-constructed transitional sentence: (1) the sermonic interrogative (one of the four adverbs) or an interrogative substitute (If the interrogative adverb is *how,* the interrogative substitute would be *by* followed by a verb ending in *ing;* if the interrogative adverb

8. Arthur S. Hoyt, *The Pulpit and American Life*, p. 156.

is *why,* the interrogative substitute would be *because of* followed by the key word; if the interrogative adverb is *when* or *where,* the acceptable interrogative substitutes would be *in which* or *at which*) ; (2) the proposition in as complete a form as possible; and (3) the key word, a noun in the plural that characterizes each main division of the sermon. An additional part of the transitional sentence may be the Scripture passage from which the message is drawn.

The following are three examples of the transitional process applied to an evangelistic sermon:

| | |
|---|---|
| *Scriptural Portion:* | Revelation 22:6-17 |
| *Subject:* | The second coming of Christ |
| *Theme:* | The importance of Christ's second coming |
| *Proposition:* | A study of the second coming of Christ is of crucial importance. |
| *Sermon Interrogative:* | Why? (Why is the second coming of Christ important?) |
| *Interrogative Substitute:* | Because of |
| *Key Word:* | Disclosures (a noun in the plural) |
| *Completed Transitional Sentence:* | A study of the second coming of Christ is of crucial importance because of the disclosures set forth in Revelation 22:6-17. |
| *Main Points:* | I. The promise of His coming (22:7) |
| | II. The purpose of His coming (22:12) |
| | III. The pinnacle of His coming (22:14) |
| *Sermon Title:* | "Christ Is Coming Back" |
| | |
| *Scriptural Portion:* | Philippians 4:4-7 |
| *Subject:* | Peace |

| | |
|---|---|
| *Theme:* | The peace of God |
| *Proposition:* | We can experience the peace of God. |
| *Sermon Interrogative:* | How? (How can we experience the peace of God?) |
| *Interrogative Substitute:* | By obeying |
| *Key Word:* | commands (a noun in the plural) |
| *Completed Transitional Sentence:* | We can experience the peace of God by obeying the commands set forth in Philippians 4:4-7. |
| *Main Points:* | I. Continue rejoicing in the Lord (4:4). |
| | II. Continue letting your moderation be known to all men (4:5). |
| | III. Stop continuing to be unduly concerned with the cares of life (4:6*a*). |
| | IV. Continue making your requests known to God (4:6*b*). |
| *Sermon Title:* | "Prescription for Peace" |

| | |
|---|---|
| *Scriptural Portion:* | 1 Peter 1:3-5 |
| *Subject:* | Regeneration |
| *Theme:* | Regeneration brings encouragement |
| *Proposition:* | A study of the doctrine of Christian regeneration can bring encouragement to each of us in an age of discouragement. |
| *Sermon Interrogative:* | Why? (Why does Christian regeneration bring encouragement?) |
| *Interrogative Substitute:* | Because of |
| *Key Word:* | benefits (a noun in the plural) |
| *Completed Transitional Sentence:* | A study of the doctrine of Christian regeneration can bring encouragement to each of us in an age of discouragement because of the benefits set forth in 1 Peter 1:3-5. |

| | |
|---|---|
| *Main Points:* | I. The Christian has a living hope (1:3). |
| | II. The Christian has an imperishable inheritance (1:4). |
| | III. The Christian has divine protection daily (1:5). |
| *Sermon Title:* | "What God Has Done" |

## E. THE BODY OF AN EVANGELISTIC SERMON

After constructing the rhetorical bridge between the explanation and the main points, the sermonizer is ready to develop the body of his evangelistic sermon. The need for a well-organized body of carefully thought-out material with meaningful divisions was negatively stated by Finney: "Lest your sermon should make a saving impression, announce no distinct propositions or heads, that will be remembered, to disturb the consciences of your hearers. . . . Avoid a logical division and subdivision of your subject, lest you should too thoroughly instruct your people."[9]

Most writers agree that an evangelistic sermon body should have at least two, but not more than five, main points. Andrew Blackwood pointed out that well-known radio evangelist Walter A. Maier was a great two-point preacher. Usually his first point was an exposition of the text, and his second was an application to the individual lives of the listeners. Most evangelistic preachers, however, need to personalize the biblical truth after each main point so that their audiences will maintain interest and attention.

The main divisions in an evangelistic message should adequately develop the subject under consideration. They should be so constructed that they throw additional light on the subject at hand. The main points should be worded in such a way that they "milk" the preaching portion of all its contents. People should know more about the passage under considera-

9. Charles G. Finney, "Preaching So As to Convert Nobody," in *Eminent Authors on Effective Revival Preaching*, ed. Walter P. Doe, p. 53.

tion when they leave the service than they knew when they entered. The main points ought to be in progressive series, one building upon the other. The progression of thought should be logical and orderly, leading ultimately to a climax. The main divisions should be natural and readily observable from the preaching text itself when called to the attention of the people. They also ought to be clear and symmetrical. Alliteration should be used meaningfully. The only time it is better not to alliterate the main points is when the alliteration might blur the meaning intended by the text. Furthermore, the wording in the main points should support the key word that has been used in the transitional sentence. For example, if the key word in the transitional sentence is "lessons," all the main points should be lessons, not warnings or commands or anything else. Equally important, the main points ought to be amplifications of the proposition and ought to repeatedly tie into it. "Each main division," as Whitesell said, "should root back into the proposition just as main branches unite with the trunk of a tree."[10] On the other hand, the main divisions should be significantly different; that is, they should not overlap to the extent that they merely say the same thing with somewhat different phraseology. The main points should be logical and capable of being remembered by the listeners.

The subdivisions of an evangelistic sermon should not be more than three or four. Too many will blur the importance of the main point. The subdivisions should seek to develop the main points through definition, clarification, or amplification. Appropriate illustrations should be interspersed within the subdivisions, along with a closing subpoint of application. The subpoint of application should personalize the content of the preaching portion by making it "live" in the everyday experiences of the hearers. As was true of the main divisions, the subdivisions should also be logical, natural, symmetrical, and progressive.

10. Whitesell, p. 47.

R. A. Torrey said that the best way to select main points is to study and analyze the biblical text thoroughly. He suggested that that can best be done by asking "who," "what," "how," and "why" questions regarding the data of the text. He gave four rules for formulating a good and properly arranged outline:

1. Make your points in logical order. . . .
2. Do not make your strongest points first and then taper down to the weakest. . . .
3. Put that point last that leads to the important decision that you have in view in your sermon. . . .
4. Give your points in such a way that the first leads naturally to the second, and the second to the third, and the third to the fourth, etc.[11]

## F. THE EVANGELISTIC INTRODUCTION

After one has constructed the body of his evangelisitc sermon with logical main points and subpoints, he is ready to formulate his introduction. Often preachers have begun the sermonic arrangement by writing the introduction first, before even analyzing the text carefully. This fundamental mistake is the reason evangelistic introductions (in many cases) are isolated and unrelated sermonettes tacked on to the body of the sermon rather than integral parts of the total message.

The characteristics of an effective evangelistic introduction are worthy of consideration. The ability to capture attention is probably the most important characteristic. The first statement the evangelist utters often sets the pace for the entire sermon. It must arouse curiosity and eager anticipation. It should strike fire.

The introduction also ought to be brief. Spurgeon put it this way: "As a rule, do not make the introduction too long. It is always a pity to build a great porch to a little house. The introduction should have something striking in it. It is well

11. Torrey, pp. 334-35.

to fire a startling shot as a signal gun to clear the decks for action."[12]

Third, the evangelistic introduction ought to be life-related. Jordan, in his *Preaching During a Revolution,* said that in the introduction the preacher ought to get on the level of his congregation. He should put himself in their shoes, so to speak. The best way to do that is to have a secular introduction—something extremely human with which people can readily identify. As Philips Brooks used to say, "Begin where the people are and lead them to the foot of the cross." The evangelistic introduction should meet people where they are and then lead into a well-organized body of truth that will take them where they ought to be. For example, if one were to bring a message on the "new birth," he could begin by speaking of natural birth as one of the great moments in life, especially in the lives of a father and mother. From there he could move into a discussion of the significance of the new birth as taught by our Lord in John 3.

Careful preparation should characterize an evangelistic introduction. "Eliminate all false starts such as apologies, anecdotes, puns, and inane remarks," Whitesell said. "Stand up, look the people in the eyes, wait a few seconds, and then either quote your text and give the first sentence of the introduction; or begin with the introduction and lead up to the text."[13]

Finally, the introduction should be direct. It should be addressed to the main point of the sermon. Its appropriateness for the sermon should be self-evident to the listener in the congregation.

There are many sources a preacher can draw upon for an effective evangelistic introduction. He can attract the attention of the hearers with a dramatic description of the circumstances of the text. Or he can relate an interesting experience that has happened to him or to someone else. He might re-

12. Charles Spurgeon, "How to Obtain and Retain the Attention of Our Hearers" in Doe, p. 236.
13. Whitesell, *Evangelistic Preaching and the Old Testament,* p. 43.

count a newspaper or magazine article that is of current significance, describe some masterpiece of art he has just seen, or speak of some recent scientific discovery. He might quote statistics to establish a strong case for practicing that which he is about to advocate. For example, if he is preaching on the subject "Paul's painful passion for the perishing" (Rom. 9:1-5), he may want to quote some of the latest population statistics and contrast them with the number of people who are not being reached for Christ. The thoughtful preacher will devote much time to the formulation of an introduction that is logical, coherent, relevant, and direct. The evangelist should not be afraid to let his people know that his introduction is factual and scholarly.

The preacher should never allow people to anticipate or expect his opening lines. The first sentence of an evangelistic introduction may take any one of various forms. The "approach sentence" may be in the form of a rhetorical question or a startling statement that is controversial. It may be a quotation from history, science, or literature. It may be in the form of an illustration—a pithy story or a humorous anecdote. (If this form is used, the humor must be related to the purpose of the sermon. Humor for the sake of humor detracts from a well-organized and carefully arranged sermon.)

## G. THE EVANGELISTIC CONCLUSION

After the sermonizer has formulated an appropriate evangelistic introduction, he next must arrange an equally significant conclusion, one that is an asset to the sermon, not a liability. A fitting conclusion is the difference between a sermon and a lecture. As Torrey put it:

> A true sermon does not exist for itself. This . . . is the great fault with many of our modern sermonizers. The sermon exists for itself as a work of art, but it is not worth anything in the line of doing good. As a work of rhetorical art it is perfect, but as a real sermon it is a total failure. What did

it accomplish? A true sermon exists for the purpose of leading someone to Christ or building some one up in Christ.[14]

A well-planned conclusion enables the preacher to make further application of the main points in the body of his message. In his concluding comments, he once again can direct the truth of the passage to the minds of his audience. The conclusion also enables the sermonizer to gather the main thoughts of the message into one giant thrust that will leave a lasting impression on the hearer. Finally, the conclusion makes it possible for the hearer to respond in an appropriate manner. Stanfield's advice is noteworthy: "In a strictly evangelistic sermon the conclusion and the invitation are one. They are not two separate things. However, the emphasis may be different, and the emphasis in a sermon should be the primary thrust of the conclusion."[15]

The evangelistic conclusion ought to be brief. A compact and concentrated conclusion will be far more effective than a protracted one. Moreover, the sermonizer should resist the temptation to include new material in his conclusion unless it is built into the context of his preaching portion. The evangelist should not employ the word *finally* as an indication to his audience that he has just received his second wind.

Second, the evangelistic conclusion should not be forced. The preacher should not have a stereotyped conclusion for every sermon that appeals first to the saved and then to the unsaved, or vice versa.

Third, the conclusion to an evangelistic sermon should be marked by strength, or intensity. As Stanfield pointed out, "Intensity does not mean loudness. Some of the most intense sermon conclusions are quiet."[16] Simplicity, sincerity, naturalness, and sermonic relatedness are also key ingredients of a decisive and effective evangelistic conclusion. Whitesell's paraphrase of G. Campbell Morgan has present-day validity in

14. Torrey, p. 337.
15. V. L. Stanfield, *Effective Evangelistic Preaching*, pp. 23-24.
16. Ibid., p. 24.

summarizing this point: "The conclusion must conclude, include, and preclude. It must positively conclude the message, must include the spiritual and moral impact and appeal of what has been said, and must preclude the possibility that our hearers escape from the message."[17]

James Hoppin defined three kinds of conclusions appropriate for the evangelistic sermon. The first is recapitulation, that is, the reassertion of the main points of the message, not in the same form or language as employed in the sermonic body, but in a fresh, vibrant form that captures the heart and mind of the listener. Applicatory inferences and remarks constitute Hoppin's second category of conclusions, inferences being logical deductions from the argument; remarks are natural suggestions drawn from it. Regarding inferences and remarks, Hoppin said:

> They should be drawn directly from the whole character and development of the sermon.
> They should be forcible, and drawn from the body of the sermon.
> They should have regard to the character and states of mind of the hearers, as well as to the character and design of the subject. . . .
> They should increase in force and importance.

The third kind of conclusion defined by Hoppin is the appeal to the feelings. The more spontaneous and natural this kind of conclusion is, Hoppin said, the better it will be for the entire evangelistic address.[18]

Weldon Crossland suggested some one-sentence appeals that can be used effectively at the close of an evangelistic sermon:

> Accept God's plan for your life.
> Follow Christ and His way.
> Bring your life into line with the high purposes of God.
> Give Christ your love, your loyalty, and your allegiance.

17. Whitesell, *Evangelistic Preaching and the Old Testament*, p. 49.
18. James Hoppin, "The Conclusion," in Doe, pp. 227-31.

Let Christ take care of all the fears, hate, sickness, and frustrations that plague your life.

Make Christ and loyalty to Him the center of your life.

Begin a new way of life now in partnership with the Son of God.

With Christ's help you can be free from your sins and evil habits.

Begin today your friendship with the divine Friend.

Let God's power transform and strengthen your life.[19]

In addition to these suggestions on how to formulate an effective conclusion, the evangelist can employ a striking, life-related incident that makes the man in the pew ready for action.

## H. THE EVANGELISTIC INVITATION

The evangelistic sermon has been known primarily by the invitation that often accompanies it. Definitively, the sermonic invitation is that part of the message that issues a challenge to the congregation to act positively upon what the preacher has proclaimed from the Word of God. Baumann, quoting Clifton J. Allen, offered this definition:

> The invitation is not a gimmick to catch souls. It is not a fetish to insure results. It is not a ritual to confirm orthodoxy. It is simply the call of Christ to confront persons with the offer of his redemption, the demands of his lordship, and the privilege of his service.[20]

Davis expressed the sentiments of almost all the writers in the field of evangelistic and homiletic theory when he said: "The most important factor . . . in the evangelistic sermon is the direct drive for a decision in favor of the message on the part of the hearers."[21] The importance of an invitation was expressed by Leighton Ford:

19. Weldon Crossland, *How to Increase Church Membership and Attendance*, p. 34.
20. J. Daniel Baumann, *An Introduction to Contemporary Preaching*, p. 209.
21. Ozora S. Davis, *Evangelistic Preaching*, p. 67.

I am convinced that the giving of some kind of public invitation to come to Christ is not only theologically correct, but also emotionally sound. Men need this opportunity for expression. The inner decision for Christ is like driving a nail through a board. The open declaration of it is like clinching the nail on the other side, so that it is not easily pulled out. Impression with expression can lead to depression.[22]

There are many reasons for giving evangelistic invitations. First, an appropriate invitation is biblical. Our Lord Himself uttered pleadingly, "Come unto me, all ye that labour and are heavy laden, and I will give you rest. Take my yoke upon you, and learn of me; for I am meek and lowly in heart: and ye shall find rest unto your souls" (Matt. 11:28-29). The New Testament record closes with a great invitation: "And the Spirit and the bride say, Come. And let him that heareth say, Come. And let him that is athirst come. And whosoever will, let him take the water of life freely" (Rev. 22:27). From an Old Testament viewpoint, Roland Leavell in *Prophetic Preaching Then and Now* said that the Old Testament prophets also pressed for a decision. He likened them to the evangelists of today and said that they made their appeals to the intellects, emotions, and wills of their hearers. For example, the prophet Elijah, in the incident on Mount Carmel in which he called fire down from heaven, urged the people to make a decision: "How long halt ye between two opinions? If the LORD be God, follow him: but if Baal, then follow him" (1 Kings 18:21). Leavell considered Elijah to be a "sensational" evangelist by today's standards. Amos, in like manner, uttered great warnings to Israel about God's impending judgment on their perpetual sinning and then said, "Prepare to meet thy God" (Amos 4:12*b*). Here, in Amos, was a model for the hell-fire-and-damnation evangelist. Hosea, in pleading for the people of the Lord to return to Him and accept His forgiving grace, said, "Take with you words, and turn to the LORD: say

22. Ford, p. 124.

107

unto him, Take away all iniquity, and receive us graciously" (Hos. 14:2). In Leavell's mind, Hosea was an "emotional" evangelist.

On the other hand, the prophet Isaiah appealed to his hearers' intellectual and reasoning powers in declaring that God would help the sincere sinner think through his need of redemption: "Come now, and let us reason together, saith the LORD: though your sins be as scarlet, they shall be as white as snow; though they be red like crimson, they shall be as wool" (Isa. 1:18). To Leavell, Isaiah was the "scholarly" evangelist or seminary professor. Finally, we have the example of Ezekiel, the shepherding pastor, who alternated consolations with warnings. He would lash out hard and then graciously appeal by urging Israel to "cast away from you all your transgressions, whereby ye have transgressed; and make you a new heart and a new spirit: for why will ye die, O house of Israel?" (Ezek. 18:31). Here, in Ezekiel, is an ideal example of the "pastor-evangelist."[23]

Second, evangelistic invitations are psychological. Whitesell explained, "Emotions aroused and desires stirred will soon pass away unless acted upon at once. Good impulses are harder to generate the second time than they were the first time if the first impulse did not result in action."[24]

Third, an evangelistic invitation is essential to the well-being of the man in the pew. As has already been mentioned, to bring a person to the point of commitment without giving him an opportunity to make a commitment may be spiritually suicidal.

Fourth, the evangelistic invitation has been a historically proved method of bringing men to Christ. Almost without exception, the great evangelistic preachers, both past and present, have used some form of invitation in securing the results of their messages.

23. Roland Leavell, *Prophetic Preaching Then and Now*, pp. 85-86.
24. Faris D. Whitesell, *Sixty-Five Ways to Give Evangelistic Invitations*, p. 17.

Last, invitations are practical in that they help achieve the main end of the gospel, namely, the salvation of the lost.

There are three issues involved in calling for a decision. The first is the theological issue. Leighton Ford has pointed out that two outstanding evangelical preachers, the late Dr. Donald Grey Barnhouse and Dr. Martyn Lloyd-Jones, avoided public decision-making, considering it to be inconsistent with the doctrines of man's inability, grace, and God's election. Though Lloyd-Jones agreed in his book on preaching that theology is the crux of the problem, he did not think that it is the complete problem; for, as he observed, even a staunch Arminian like John Wesley chose not to make use of the "altar call" method.[25]

The second issue is the emotional issue. Dr. Ford believes that one must distinguish between emotionalism and emotion: Emotionalism is emotion isolated, emotion for emotion's sake. There is a legitimate place for emotion in preaching the Gospel. Nothing truly human lacks emotion.[26]

Furthermore, the evangelist must recognize the danger of an emotional decision. Normally, such a decision will result in a constant attempt to reproduce the emotional state—thus in an unbalanced Christian life—or in a feeling of betrayal, suspicion, and reaction against any religious experience at all. Therefore, although emotions are vitally important, one must appeal to the whole man—intellect, conscience, emotion, and will (see Mark 12:30).

The third issue in giving an invitation is the practical one. This issue involves the danger, on the one hand, of having no method of bringing people to Christ, and the opposite danger of overusing one method to the point of "boxing-up" and limiting the Holy Spirit in our preconceived practices.

There are many different kinds, or variations, of the invitation that the preacher can use:

25. D. Martyn Lloyd-Jones, *Preaching and Preachers*, p. 270.
26. Ford, pp. 122-23.

*The age-group invitation:* Here the evangelist in advance selects various people within the congregation who have come to Christ at different ages—age ten, fifteen, twenty, and so on. When the evangelist mentions that some people come to Christ at a certain age, the person preselected will step out first and then others his same age will follow him to an altar of prayer.

*The altar-call invitation:* The song leader leads the congregation in an invitatory hymn while the evangelist pleads with people to come to Christ. People are encouraged to come forward and kneel at the altar, where other Christians deal with them. This kind of invitation often leads into the aftermeeting, in which there are testimonies and songs sung in praise to God for what He has done in the lives of the new converts.

*The Bible-verse invitation:* All Christians are invited to stand and quote John 3:16 together with the evangelist. While the Christians remain standing, the evangelist invites all those who would like to join this Christian company to stand and come forward.

*The Christians-lead-the-way invitation:* The evangelist asks Christians to come forward and pray for the unconverted. As they pray, the unsaved are asked to respond.

*The contact-the-pastor invitation:* The evangelist invites the people who have been helped by the message to contact the pastor, either at the close of the service or during the week, to talk over their decision for Christ or to receive more counsel.

*The decision-within-the-heart invitation:* This is made quite apart from any outward display and is usually implicit in the closing prayer, wherein the preacher asks the Lord to help the people practice the truth of the message during the coming week.

*The discussion-and-debate invitation:* This was the method of Dr. James Reid, who invited his congregation to the hall in his church after an evangelistic sermon to encourage dialogue about the message. Both the saved and the unsaved could ask questions and exchange ideas.

110

*The inquiry-room invitation:* The evangelist invites all who want to make a commitment to Christ to come forward so that they can be directed to an adjoining room for prayer and spiritual counsel by trained leaders.

*The judge-and-jury invitation:*

> Speak on, "What think ye of Christ." Weigh the evidence for and against Christ. Introduce a few well-known enemies of Jesus and quote their testimony. These will usually include the Pharisees, Pilate and his wife, the thief on the cross, the centurion, and Judas. Then present the witness of such friends as John the Baptist, Matthew, Mark, Luke, John, Thomas, and Peter. Present these witnesses as though they actually came to the platform and bore their witness.
>
> After the message, the audience is told that it is the jury and must render a verdict. Those who believe that Christ was an impostor and not what he claimed to be are invited to stand. None ever stand on this invitation, but it electrifies the congregation. The preacher then asks all who believe Christ is what the Bible says He is, the very Son of God and the Saviour of mankind, to stand. Almost everybody will immediately and dramatically stand. Express appreciation for their vote of confidence in Christ. Tell them that everybody who believes about him should accept him as Saviour. Invite those who have not made such a commitment to come.[27]

*The pray-it-through invitation:* The evangelist asks for no visible response but exhorts those who have been deeply touched to go home and think and pray over the message until they have made their peace with God.

*The prayer-object invitation:* In this instance, all the Christians who are praying specifically for some unsaved person are asked to stand. While they continue in prayer, the evangelist asks all those who believe that they may be the objects of prayer to stand, indicating that they, too, are concerned about the destiny of their souls.

27. W. E. Grindstaff, *Ways to Win,* p. 196.

*The progressive invitation:* Here the preacher gives one invitation and then moves on to another invitation that is completely different. The problem with this kind of invitation is that it tends to become so broad and general that everyone in the congregaiton thinks that he should be at the altar.

*The raised-hands invitation:* Just before he closes the meeting in prayer, the evangelist asks all those whose hearts have been touched by the Holy Spirit to raise their hands for prayer. He then prays, asking God to help them obey the message and respond to Christ.

*The remain-seated invitation:* The congregation remains seated while the invitatory hymn is sung, and honest seekers may get up out of their seats and come to Christ on their own.

*The report-of-decision invitation:* People are encouraged to remain in their seats to make their decisions for Christ. After an indefinite period of time, they are urged to come forward and report to the evangelist the decisions they have made.

*The sign-the-card invitation:* In this case, the people in the congregation are urged to sign a card, indicating the kind of decision they have made, and hand it to the pastor as they leave the service. The evangelist can then follow up during the week on those who handed in cards.

*The standing invitation:* Those who have made decisions for Christ are invited to stand as a silent witness to the new-found faith.

*The testimony invitation:* Christians may be asked to give a three or four minute testimony of their faith in Christ, after which an invitation to come to Christ is given to those who are not believers.

*The visualized invitation:* In this kind of invitation, religious photographs, slides, or movies are projected upon a large screen in the front of the auditorium, with printed invitations on them. People are urged to come forward in the semidarkness of the room to make their peace with Christ. Realistically, the invitation at any given service may involve a combination of any of the various kinds just discussed.

The invitation, to be persuasive, must be tied in closely with the major thrust of the sermon. In other words, it should be carefully planned and written out. It should grow out of the main theme of the message so that the people will not be surprised when it is given. Baumann agreed with this opinion, stating that the invitation should be "consistent with the sermon and its theme, . . . prepared in advance, and given simply, clearly, and compassionately. People should know exactly what they are responding to."[28] Consequently, if one's sermonic emphasis is on the salvation of sinners, the invitation will be directed toward the lost. If the thrust is on Christian stewardship with reference to time, talent, and treasure, the invitation should challenge the people to tithe and give of their time and talent to the service of the Lord.

Although the invitation should grow out of the sermonic theme, Brown, Clinard, and Northcutt also explained that the minister has a responsibility to minister to all the needs in his congregation. Therefore, after appealing to the groups of people for which his sermon was primarily intended, the preacher may, through careful observation of his audience and the leading of the Spirit, make other appeals, secondary to his main one. For example, if his main objective was the salvation of sinners, he may also appeal to his church's youth to surrender their lives to God in total discipleship or summon backsliders to return to the fold. As a general rule, however, the preacher must present only one invitation at a time. To state many all at once only confuses the congregation and limits the Spirit of God needlessly. As a result, when the preacher feels led to make additional appeals, he must do so unrushed and in a spirit of love and concern. At other times, because of the nature of the congregation, the shortness of the time, or the size of the audience, the preacher may have to announce various appeals within a brief period of time without allowing

28. Baumann, pp. 209-10.

113

time between appeals for appropriate response. In such cases, the minister should adequately explain each alternative so that the audience can respond intelligently.[29]

Ozora Davis, in his *Evangelistic Preaching,* made remarks in accord with Brown, Clinard, and Northcutt, but from a slightly different perspective. In his mind, "More important than any single act of decision . . . is the persuasive element of the sermon as a whole. The evangelistic sermon must be simply keyed to the note of invitation and persuasion."[30] In other words, the invitation should not only be an outgrowth of the sermonic theme, but it should also be implicit throughout the entire sermon.

Persuasion is accomplished not only through letting the invitation grow out of the sermon, but also through purposefully choosing the content of the message. To do this, one must preach on the great and moving themes of the Bible. The preacher must vividly confront unbelievers with the illogic of their position by pointing out on one hand the results of sin and, on the other hand, the resources and power that they can have through faith in Christ. He must point out that God cannot be eluded indefinitely and that only Christ can make the guilty guiltless. He must hold up Christ as the All-Sufficient One and make the cross the center of his appeal.

Persuasion is also accomplished by being aware of the various appeals that move people. Dr. Charles Koller said:

> The preacher, in every legitimate appeal from the pulpit, is addressing himself to the hearer's conscience. Conscience is the awareness of the voice of God speaking through the Holy Spirit to the soul—instructing, encouraging, approving; or correcting, warning, rebuking. To preach without reliance upon the cooperation of the Holy Spirit through the voice of conscience would be sheer presumption. But while every

29. H. C. Brown, Jr., H. Gordon Clinard, and Jesse J. Northcutt, *Steps to the Sermon,* pp. 131-32.
30. Davis, p. 69.

114

Biblical appeal is ultimately an appeal to conscience, there are many roads to the heart.[31]

Dr. Koller went on to list seven such appeals, or roads, to the heart—the appeals to altruism, aspiration, curiosity, duty, fear, love, and reason. George Sweazey enlarged on that number by suggesting twenty evangelistic appeals—appeals to the sense of sin, dread of impersonal forces, lost assurances, anxiety, boredom, self-perplexity, death, loneliness, the sense of something lacking, hunger for truth, the missing significance of God, mistrust of life, inner conflict, resentment of material domination, eagerness for a better world, the appeal of the heroic, the craving for brotherhood, love of home and family, admiration for Jesus Christ, and the power of the cross.[32] To these appeals Stanfield added the appeals to the basic drives inherent in individuals, such as self-preservation; personal happiness; recognition, or prestige; security; freedom; adventure; and satisfaction.[33] After touching on one of these basic drives and making his appeal, the preacher can use the persuasion principle that there is a good to be gained or an evil to be avoided. Stanfield listed sixteen contrasts to visualize his point:

| | |
|---|---|
| Assurance | Fear |
| Fellowship | Loneliness |
| Purpose | Lack of Meaning |
| Peace | Inner Conflict |
| Strength | Weakness |
| Certainty | Uncertainty |
| Changeless | Changing |
| Forgiveness | Guilt |
| Heaven | Hell |
| Eternal Life | Eternal Separation |
| Life | Death |
| At Home | Away from Home |

31. Charles W. Koller, *Expository Preaching Without Notes*, p. 108.
32. George E. Sweazey, *Effective Evangelism: The Greatest Work in the World*, pp. 60-69.
33. Stanfield, p. 32.

```
Manliness  ................... Cowardice
Fair  Play  ..................... Unfair Play
Normal  ...................... Abnormal
Reasonable  ................. Unreasonable[34]
```

There are certain appeals that the preacher may not want
to employ because they are questionable from the Christian
perspective. Such are appeals to: fear (As one minister said, "I
would rather frighten them into Heaven than let them go to
Hell unafraid.") ; conformity, or social pressure ("We want
every member of this class to join the church. You know how
happy it would make your wife.") ; worldly motives ("All the
best people in town are in our church.") ; and superstition
("pulling God down to man's purposes instead of lifting man
up to God's") .[35] Therefore, the minister must use great discretion when deciding on the appeals he will employ in any
given preaching situation.

A factor often overlooked in a consideration of persuasiveness is the time factor involved. That is, when is the best time
for making the appeal to act on the truth of the message? The
best time is at the conclusion of the message, when people are
still in their seats—not while they are standing, reaching for
the hymnbooks, taking care of the children, and, in general,
getting ready to bolt for the exits. The reason for this is obvious. Only when the evangelist has the undivided attention
of the audience can his invitation be persuasive and well understood. If there is much disturbance, the people in the
process of making a decision will be distracted from the all-
important decision at hand and turn their minds to the activity around them. By having the people remain seated, the
preacher can make clear what the response is to be for, and
then he can ask the congregation to arise, sing, and respond
accordingly.

Likewise, the evangelist must not rush into or out of the

34.  Ibid., p. 35.
35.  Sweazey, pp. 69-71.

giving of the invitation. If the invitation has been built into the central thrust of the message, adequate time will have been allowed for it, even if such planning requires that the body of the sermon be shortened, the announcements eliminated, or one congregational hymn omitted. Such actions ahead of time will help the preacher build to a persuasive and planned climax. Not only must the evangelist take pains to plan the proper amount of time for the invitation, but he must also be sensitive so that he concludes the invitation when it becomes evident that the Spirit of God has stopped working. No minister should presume on God's rights by lingering and holding on when no visible responses are made.

As to how long an invitation should be, Stanfield succinctly said: "The length of the invitation is dependent upon many factors, such as the attitude of the church, the prospects present, the spirit of the service, and the leadership of the Holy Spirit. As a general rule I gauge the length of the invitation by the response."[36]

The following pivotal marks characterize an effective evangelistic invitation:

1. The invitation should be given cautiously.

2. The invitation should be given clearly.

3. The invitation should be given compassionately.

4. The invitation should be given confidently.

5. The invitation should be given with conviction, not out of conformity to tradition.

6. The invitation should be given courageously.

7. The invitation should be given courteously. No undue pressure should be brought to bear upon an individual, making him incapable of reaching a rational decision on the basis of his own volition.

36. Stanfield, p. 37.

8. The invitation should be given dependently. The serious, responsible evangelist must abandon all professional gimmicks and psychological tricks. He must give the invitation out of a confident trust in the power of a limitless God.

9. The invitation should be given earnestly.

10. The invitation should be given with empathy.

11. The invitation should be given with expectancy. If the preacher does not expect God to honor His Word with a positive response, there probably will be none. Jesus said, "According to your faith be it unto you" (Matt. 9:29).

12. The invitation should be given firmly, with no fumbling or timidity.

13. The invitation should be given in a friendly manner, not oratorically.

14. The invitation should be given gently, with no high-pressure techniques or dominating methods.

15. The invitation should be given honestly.

16. The invitation should be given with absolute integrity. Make the implications clear-cut. Do not be guilty of saying, "We shall sing only one more verse," and then singing five more.

17. The invitation should be given naturally. Do not try to be someone else. Be yourself, but be your best self.

18. The invitation should be given optimistically.

19. The invitation should be given pleadingly (without begging).

20. The invitation should be given positively:

Never permit a doubt to enter your invitation. It is often

fatal to begin an invitation by saying, "If there are any present who may possibly care to confess Christ." It is better to begin with the note of certainty: "While singing the following hymn, those who intend making their great decision and confession tonight will quietly and reverently leave their pews and come to the front."[37]

21. The invitation should be given prayerfully.

22. The invitation should be given repeatedly. Said Sweazey,

Experience shows that if the invitation is given again it wins some who do not respond at first. People have to think it through, and often struggle it through before they are ready. Sin and the habit of postponement are hard to get around.[38]

23. The invitation should be given resourcefully:

Change your methods of giving the invitation. Surprise people with something new from time to time. Think over your invitation beforehand and have three or four plans in mind. When the time comes for the invitation, let the Holy Spirit guide you how to begin and how to proceed through to the end.[39]

24. The invitation should be given scripturally. Quote the Scriptures freely, and rely upon the Word to accomplish the divine purpose.

25. The invitation should be given thoroughly:

Do not stop too soon, particularly when you know people are present who should make a decision at once. Invitations should not be prolonged to the point of wearing out the audience. On the other hand, hold on as long as there is reasonable prospect of some decision.[40]

26. The invitation should be given with urgency and definiteness.

37. Lionel B. Fletcher, *The Effective Evangelist*, p. 161.
38. Sweazey, p. 175.
39. Whitesell, *Sixty-Five Ways to Give Evangelistic Invitations*, p. 27.
40. Ibid., p. 27.

27. The invitation should be given vigorously:

> Be your physical best for the invitation. Avoid being worn out, weary, fatigued, worried, preoccupied or indisposed. Concentrate all physical, mental, emotional and spiritual energies upon giving a good invitation.[41]

To summarize, the sermonic invitation, to be persuasive, must be intimately tied to the biblical message of the preaching portion. It must be well planned and thought out. Furthermore, the invitation should focus on specific appeals that the preacher chooses ahead of time on the basis of the needs of his congregation. But, most importantly, it must be issued in love and in complete reliance on the Holy Spirit.

41. Whitesell, *Sixty-Five Ways to Give Evangelistic Invitations*, p. 28.

# V

## *Sermonic Style for Evangelistic Preaching*

"NEXT TO THE BAPTISM of the Holy Spirit the most indispensable gift for every American preacher is a mastery of the English tongue. No time should be begrudged that is spent in perfecting the preacher's style," said Jefferson.[1] According to Aristotle, "Style should be characterized by perspicuity, purity, dignity and propriety."[2]

Definitively speaking, style refers to the process a sermonizer goes through as he phrases and clothes with language the ideas he has discovered through invention and organized through arrangement.

As was true with arrangement, the writers in the field of evangelistic and homiletic theory have often overlooked style. Poor style has opened up evangelistic preaching to justified criticism on the part of some. Broadus observed,

> Mere claptrap and sensationalism, tirades of cheap wit and vulgar denunciation, extreme and one-sided statements, half-truths and spurious errors—all these infect as a deadly poison a large proportion of that which is called evangelistic preaching.[3]

Hervey said, "The deepening conviction that sermons which have cost but little study have been instrumental in doing

1. Lloyd M. Perry, "Sermon Style in Contemporary Terms," in *Baker's Dictionary of Practical Theology,* ed. Ralph Turnbull, p. 74.
2. Lester Thonssen and A. Craig Baird, *Speech Criticism: The Development of Standards for Rhetorical Appraisal,* p. 69.
3. John A. Broadus, *On the Preparation and Delivery of Sermons,* p. 308.

much good has led some evangelists to neglect style, and even method."[4] This sad admission by Broadus and Hervey emphasizes the need for positive material on how a preacher can improve his evangelistic style and recognize the lasting qualities of a good evangelistic address.

## A. The Importance of Evangelistic Style

Style was an important asset to the evangelists who made their mark in the history of preaching. Two key evangelists especially known for their style were John Wesley and Charles G. Finney. Barclay quoted the stylistic philosophy of Wesley, who said of himself:

> I design plain truth for plain people; therefore, of set purpose I abstain from all nice and philosophical speculations; from all perplexed and intimate reasonings; and, as far as possible, from even the show of learning. I labor to avoid all words which are not easy to understand, all which are not used in common life; and, in particular, those kinds of technical terms that so frequently occur in Bodies of Divinty; those modes of speaking which men of reading are intimately acquainted with, but which to the common people are an unknown tongue.[5]

Finney's style coincided to a great degree with Wesley's in that he, too, ignored the religious terminology of the schools of higher learning, choosing rather to couch his sermons in the homely and everyday terms of the common man.

The importance of good sermonic style, especially with reference to the evangelistic sermon, cannot be overemphasized. It was said of Henry Clay that he made his friends with one vocabulary and lost the presidency with another. Likewise an evangelist can lose his congregation if he is not careful to develop a lucid and articulate style that crosses all the communication barriers confronting him in any given evangelistic

---

4. G. W. Hervey, *Manual of Revivals*, p. 33.
5. William Barclay, *Fishers of Men*, p. 102.

setting. To develop such a style, the preacher, as he sits at his desk preparing his sermon, must ever keep in mind the nature of the people he is addressing. He must write as he is going to speak, going over the language he uses time and again to make sure that each thought is clear, understandable, and unambiguous. As he pours over the style of his sermon, he must see to it that each word means to his audience what it means to him; if one does not, he must readily substitute for it a more accurate word. The evangelist who is concerned with style would do well to heed the admonition of Cuyler when he said, "*Begin* to preach in such a style that you shall nail every ear to the pulpit; *end* your discourse with an appeal that shall clench the truth and send your hearer home with God's Word ringing in his memory."[6]

## B. The Improvement of Evangelistic Style

Improvement of style should be the goal of every evangelistic preacher. "Status quo-itis" should be fought off. Development and improvement ought to be uppermost in the preacher's mind. An evangelist can perfect his style by avoiding the use of slang language and slipshod English. Templeton put this principle in perspective: "The goal is not accommodation to the linguistic practice of a generation but statement in terms that have meaning to the hearer."[7] Improvement also comes to evangelistic style when concise diction is used. In regard to this, Brastow's words are appropriate:

> One needs to know not only what to say, but how much and when and where, and how to stop. The adequate evangelistic sermon carries no surplus material. It eliminates padding. It wastes no words. It is dangerous to say too much. He who speaks to the feelings of his hearers may easily cause a revulsion. A little over-doing spoils the impression.[8]

6. T. L. Cuyler, "The Successful Minister," in *Eminent Authors on Effective Revival Preaching,* ed. Walter P. Doe, p. 127.
7. Charles B. Templeton, *Evangelism for Tomorrow,* pp. 103-4.
8. Lewis O. Brastow, *The Work of the Preacher: A Study of Homiletical Principles and Methods,* p. 247.

From a different viewpoint, evangelistic style can be enhanced by getting right to the main point of the message without camouflaging the real intent with anecdotes and niceties that distract the hearer, keeping him from hearing what he came to hear, namely, the gospel of Christ presented in a plain and effective manner.

The use of nontechnical language will also immensely improve evangelistic style. As has been noted already, the use of such language was one of Finney's main strengths. In his *Lectures on Revivals of Religion,* he exhorted his readers to use the "language of the common life." That is, the evangelist should use words that the members of the congregation know well and use frequently. A technical term—even if it is explained at the beginning of the sermon—is bound to be forgotten, and ultimately it can confuse people who do not usually remember the special meanings that an evangelist may attach to certain words. Finney further warned:

> If [an evangelist] uses a word in common use, but employs it in an *un*common sense, giving his special explanations, it is no better; for the people will soon forget his special explanations, and then the impression actually conveyed to their minds will be according to their *common* understanding of the word. And thus he will never convey the right idea to his congregation.[9]

The purposeful repetition of ideas can also provide improvement in the evangelist's style. To repeat key thoughts and phrases for emphasis is not a weakness but a strength. Effective repetition was one of the distinctive features characterizing the style of radio evangelist Walter A. Maier. He often repeated not only key concepts, but also imperative verbs that contributed significant insights into the biblical text. Between such repetitions he interspersed life-related facts and relevant ideas gleaned from a very wide range of reading.

9. Charles G. Finney, *Lectures on Revivals of Religion,* p. 193.

Probably one of the most helpful homiletic books from the standpoint of suggestions for improved style is the one by Henry Sloane Coffin, titled *What to Preach*. Coffin suggested that the preacher can improve his style by employing language that enables the congregation to visualize what he is saying:

> The preacher will try for language which makes his hearers *see*. All works of art—and a sermon is one of the highest forms of literary creation—awaken the imagination. A moving speaker turns men's ears into eyes. They are made to see life's situations, and situations which lie in the realm of the spirit, and made to feel themselves in them. The language which a preacher wants is that of novelists and poets and dramatists, and of writers of letters and of autobiography, who capture and exhibit the workings of the mind and heart. He has to avoid the abstract, and for this reason he must rid himself not only of the jargon of theological lecture-rooms and of most of his scholarly books, but also of their unimaginative way of putting things. He must shun such prosaic and pedestrian forms and expressions as these lectures are cast in.[10]

### C. THE QUALITIES OF EVANGELISTIC STYLE

Several qualities should characterize the style of the effective evangelistic sermon. Each quality comes as the result of work on the part of the sermonizer who sees the phrasing of words as an integral part of the sermonic process. First, the evangelistic sermon should be natural. The sermonizer should not seek to imitate the evangelistic style of another preacher. Natural style helped to make Spurgeon, Moody, Finney, and Whitefield great evangelists. Said Brastow:

> There is nothing in the discourses of these great evangelists that insures their perpetuity. But they express what is real to them and they bear the evidence of reality in their directness and pungency. A religious awakening is likely to bring

10. Henry Sloane Coffin, *What to Preach*, p. 180.

a revival of naturalness, simplicity, directness, compactness and cogency of speech.[11]

Effective evangelistic style is also known for its simplicity. Some think that simplicity of style renders an evangelistic sermon easy to formulate. Said Goodell, "If one thinks that simple, soulful words are easily spoken, and that they are the sign of lack of preparation, let him try to use them, and he will discern his mistake."[12] Coffin reminded the sermonizer:

> We have to paint life's occurrences so that our hearers seem to themselves to be living through them. We have to take out of their mouths the phrases they use.[13]

To be simple does not mean to be juvenile or unacademic. A simple style does not employ hackneyed expressions. Simplicity of style means that the sermon is couched in such terminology that even the uneducated can understand and respond to the message of the gospel. The sermon is to be so well understood by all that none can mistake its significance except willfully.

Life-relatedness is a third important quality of evangelistic style that must be developed. The language the preacher employs should be contemporary and readily recognizable by the average man or woman. The phraseology used should be in terms of present needs and problems. Jesus Himself used a language of life that confronted people where they were and then awakened positive response. The people always knew what He was talking about because He used a terminology that was familiar to them.

Evangelistic style should be clear and understandable. It is said that Sangster liked the inspired misquotation, "Though I speak with the tongues of men and angels and have not clarity, I am become as sounding brass and tinkling cymbal."

Albert Barnes rightly asserted "The hopes of the Gospel are

11. Brastow, pp. 246-47.
12. Charles L. Goodell, *Pastoral and Personal Evangelism*, p. 108.
13. Coffin, pp. 181-82.

so clear that there is no need of ambiguity or enigma; no need of abstruse metaphysical reasoning in the pulpit."[14] A clear style omits all irrelevancies and speculations that have no direct bearing on the subject at hand. A sermon that is not clear is of no use to the people in the congregation. In fact, a sermon that is not understandable is really an indictment against the preacher. Porter said, "Strange, and obscure terms in the pulpit, argue more for the pride and conceit of the minister, than for his piety or good taste. They strongly indicate that the conversion of the people is not his object, or that he is deficient in judgment."[15] Again, a clear style does not employ Greek and Latin phrases that may seem, from the evangelist's point of view, to put the academic stamp on the message, but which only confuse the congregation. Finney said that he had heard some revivalistic preachers whose language was so far over the heads of the people that if the latter had not come equipped with dictionaries, they would not have understood at all. Of such an obscure style Finney said, "So many phrases were brought in, manifestly to adorn the discourse, rather than to instruct the people that I have felt as if I wanted to tell the man, 'Sit down, and not confound the people's minds with your *barbarian* preaching, that they cannot understand.' "[16]

Cultivating a personal style will also be advantageous for the evangelistic preacher. Weatherspoon, in his work *Sent Forth to Preach,* said that this was especially demonstrated in the apostolic, evangelistic preaching of Peter, Stephen, and Paul. What they preached represented their personal beliefs as based upon the revealed Word of God, and their sermons were often openly autobiographical. This quality of style, however, must not be abused. Such abuse arises when the preacher sets himself up as a worthy personal example to fol-

14. Albert Barnes, "Clearness of Style in Preaching," in Doe, p. 68.
15. James Porter, *Revivals of Religion,* p. 78.
16. Finney, p. 193.

127

low. Nevertheless, personal experience, used with discretion, can be very effective.

The evangelistic preacher should seek to develop an educational style. He must appeal not only to the emotions but also to the mind of the listener. This can be done in a clear and understandable manner. Paul S. Rees in *Stir Up the Gift* was right in labeling as fallacy the assertion that evangelism and education are incompatible.

The emphatic quality is also an important aspect of evangelistic style. Not only should the preacher have his hearers before him as he prepares, but he should also put himself "in their shoes." How would he respond if he were in the pew rather than in the pulpit? An empathic style makes for a sympathetic audience. People will respond more readily if the preacher's words let them know that he has been in their situation.

An animated, or conversational, style is a key quality in evangelistic preaching. Being able to converse with one's audience rather than just talk at them is a noble quality. In our day, Billy Graham evidences such a conversational quality, especially in his use of rhetorical questions. It is interesting that a conversational style was promoted by Finney even though many of his predecessors were opposed to it. Said Finney:

> [Style] should be conversational. Preaching, to be understood should be colloquial in its style. A minister must preach just as he would talk, if he wishes to be fully understood. Nothing is more calculated to make a sinner feel that religion is some mysterious thing that he cannot understand, than this mouthing, formal, lofty style of speaking so generally employed in the pulpit. The minister ought to do as the lawyer does when he wants to make a jury understand him perfectly. He uses a style perfectly colloquial. This lofty, swelling style will do no good. The gospel will never

produce any great effects, until ministers *talk to* their hearers, in the pulpit, as they talk in private conversation.[17]

Henry Sloane Coffin said that evangelistic style is partly a moral quality:

> [It is] a resolve to portray what one feels so that one's hearers feel it, an abnegation of slovenly and slipshod diction, a refusal to clutter up sentences with phrases which do not stand for actualities, a passion for the exact and comely word. And it is partly a gift of the imagination, bestowed in varying measures, sometimes dulled and sometimes enhanced by culture.[18]

Style should also be biblical. That is, the preacher should not be afraid to use biblical terminology in his sermon. It is interesting to note that Finney expressed the same concern that many present-day preachers and theologians are expressing about technical biblical words and phrases such as *regeneration* and *sanctification*; namely, they are often alluded to but seldom defined. The only way to help people understand technical biblical terms is to define and explain them when they are employed in any given evangelistic sermon. Rather than avoiding the use of biblical words and theological concepts, the effective evangelist will employ them sparingly, explaining them in everyday terminology and using some pertinent, life-related illustrations.

Evangelistic style should be direct and fearless. Andrew Blackwood observed:

> The man in the pulpit is no mere essayist who has been rambling about in a garden and plucking beautiful flowers so as to bedeck the Cross. He is an ambassador from King Christ, with a message that calls for decision, here and now. Would the ambassador from the Court of Saint James tone down the words of his monarch? No! In like manner, with-

17. Ibid., p. 192.
18. Coffin, p. 182.

129

out being abrupt or tactless, the soul-winning preacher addresses the man in the pew.[19]

Finally, urgency should be evident in evangelistic style. As one clothes his sermon with words, he should endeavor to win the wills of his audience. This may be accomplished by appealing either to the intellect or to the emotions. Again, Blackwood is helpful:

> As a rule the first portion of the message is chiefly to the intellect; the latter part may be more to the emotions. But in the fine art of preaching all our rules break down. The main thing is to have a message from God and then preach it with a soul on fire. According to Father Taylor, the evangelist to seamen, the preacher must "take something hot out of his own heart and shove it into mine."[20]

19. Andrew W. Blackwood, *Evangelism in the Home Church*, p. 86.
20. Ibid., p. 88.

# VI

## Sermonic Presentation and Evangelistic Preaching

THE DELIVERY, or presentation, of the gospel message has received the greatest attention of the writers in the field of evangelistic and homiletic theory. Delivery is the final aspect of the rhetorical process. Its importance cannot be overemphasized, for ideas discovered (invention), organized (arrangement), phrased (style), and retained (memory) must be properly presented, or else all that has gone before will be for naught (except for the preacher's own spiritual well-being). Etter summarized well the importance of the evangelistic delivery when he said of the preacher:

> He should glow and melt with the solemnity of his theme; should grapple with men's consciences, and speak with the animation of direct appeal and of earnest expostulation. An ice-lump in the pulpit will make the whole congregation a moral refrigerator. People can not get warm around a cold stone.[1]

### A. PSYCHOLOGICAL FACTORS IN DELIVERY

Of the many factors involved in evangelistic delivery, psychology plays a key role. One element in the psychology of evangelistic sermonic delivery is persuasion. In its generic sense, persuasion

1. John W. Etter, *The Preacher and His Sermon*, p. 248.

is any verbal method of influencing human conduct. In its specific meaning we refer to influencing human conduct by emotional appeals. It is the instilling, activating, or directing in another individual or other individuals a belief or a type of conduct recommended by the speaker. It was Aristotle who said that there were three sources of persuasive effectiveness. The first, the logical, refers to the facts in the logic of the subject matter. The second, the pathetic, refers to the emotions, biases, and opinions of the audience. The third, the ethical, involves the speaker's personality. These three have been referred to as logos, pathos, and ethos.[2]

To be persuasive, the evangelistic delivery must be authoritative, enthusiastic, and earnest. It must endeavor to conquer the will of the listener and lead to transformation of life.

Motivation is another important psychological factor to consider in designing and developing an effective evangelistic delivery. There is a difference between motivation and manipulation, as Craig Skinner noted:

> Preachers are representatives rather than salesmen. We represent Christ, standing in His place as ambassadors proclaiming reconciliation. Persons need to become aware of their need to become Christ-like through their meeting with transformed pulpit personalities. They are not to be forced into a Christian commitment through cleverly presented promotion. The preacher who sells salvation, *manipulates*. The preacher who presents genuine values, and guides their exchange for the benefit of his hearer, merely *motivates*. Manipulation involves force; motivation bases on insight.[3]

"The most important study in evangelistic preaching is perhaps the study of motive, or a study of the various methods by which the will is moved," said Brastow.[4] He suggested six possible motives that are apt to affect evangelistic delivery:

2. Lloyd M. Perry, *Biblical Preaching for Today's World*, pp. 173-74.
3. Craig Skinner, *The Teaching Ministry of the Pulpit*, p. 109.
4. Lewis O. Brastow, *The Work of the Preacher: A Study of Homiletical Principles and Methods*, p. 247.

1. The intellectual motive. . . .

Some men are much more easily reached than others by the presentation of the truth convincingly to the mind, particularly by the presentation of Christ as the one who answers certain intellectual needs and meets their intellectual difficulties. . . .

2. The aesthetic motive. . . .

A right character is not only the realization of moral rectitude but of moral beauty. It is easy to see that the sense of an ideal goodness is both ethical and aesthetic. There are those who have a strong sense of the attractions of goodness. They carry about with them an ideal of what God intended them to be. This ideal of manhood lingers with them and haunts them. Conscience condemns them for failure to realize the standard set for them. . . .

3. The paracletic motive. . . .

The sorrows, disappointments, hardships and dissatisfactions of life prepare many for the reception of Christ as the one who brings comfort, strength, and peace. . . .

4. The emotional motive. . . .

There are those who may be reached by an appeal to fear. . . . The value of it as a motive is that it arrests for a time the wrong action of the soul and gives opportunity for other motives to take hold. But it is these other motives, operating unconsciously or half unconsciously it may be, that do the work. A man can never be simply frightened away from sin into a life of holy virtue. A love for the soul's true good itself must first spring up in the heart because it is recognized as such. One may be startled in his bad way so as to be made afraid of God. But no one is ever a changed man morally simply by being made afraid of God. One may be terrified at the consequences of sin, but if he does not come to hate it, he will not turn from it. . . .

(The opposite of an appeal to fear is an appeal to love.)

133

. . . The pathos of his [Christ's] sorrow and of his suffering love has been a mighty power in the evangelism of the church. . . .

5. The moral motive. . . .

It is possible to work directly upon the results of the early training of the conscience, upon a trained sense of obligation to Christ, in which the conscience has been precommitted. . . . The value of early religious education is conspicuous here. It creates a conscience for Christ. It precommits the moral nature and secures a bias towards him. There are those who can be reached by appeal to a certain sense of honor, to a moral sentiment and judgment that respects a character and life that are worthy of a man, and the possibilities that are opened up in Christ before them. . . .

6. The social motive. . . .

Personal example, various forms of personal influence, are powerful factors in winning men to Christ.[5]

The personal motivation of the evangelist himself is also a significant psychological factor. If the sermon does not move the preacher, it will in the same measure be powerless with the audience. Personal indifference and coldness on the part of the preacher will inevitably produce the same kind of attitude in his hearers.

The effective evangelist must be a student of the basic drives of people. It is noteworthy that the business world spends much time and energy discovering the basic needs and desires of people through surveys and opinion polls. When a definite trend has been established, businessmen cater to it to merchandise their particular products. The sermonizer must do the same thing in that he, too, must direct his message to the basic desires and needs of his people. To do that, he must appeal directly to the inherent drives of individuals. However, the preacher must also realize that an appeal that will reach

5. Brastow, pp. 248-56.

one person may not reach another. Therefore, there is a need to evaluate and reevaluate one's appeal, through personal observation and encounter, in light of the composition of the audience.

Coffin listed some appeals that can be employed in light of the basic drives of people. The evangelist, said Coffin, may appeal to spiritual alternatives, to the contrasting life-styles of the sinner and the saint, to the naturalness of faith, to the inescapable God, to the sense of futility caused by the consciousness of guilt, to the Christian philosophy of life, to the satisfaction of the Christian way of life, or to the cross of Christ as the climactic point in the history of man.[6] In all these appeals, the evangelist must aim at the intellect, emotions, and volition of the hearers.

Suggestion is a powerful psychological factor in evangelistic delivery. A thoughtful suggestion based upon biblical evidence will move men to action. Fanciful suggestions devoid of truth, however, will often raise insurmountable barriers between the pulpit and the pew.

Emotion used as a psychological factor in delivery has been very prominent in evangelistic preaching. Emotion is a vital part of the total response to truth. Pseudoemotionalism unrelated to the truth should not find its way into evangelistic preaching. Genuine emotion, however, cannot help but result from the proclamation of Christ and His claims. The evangelist who is Christ-conscious will feel deeply about the message he is delivering. Said Davis:

> The preacher wants to make his hearers feel the message; then he must feel it himself. Nothing will kindle emotion but emotion. The preacher whose voice never breaks never will see any hard hearts broken by his message. But deep feeling cannot be summoned into action at the word of command. In fact, the preacher who is not habitually earnest and moved in respect to his message will evoke only slight

6. Henry Sloane Coffin, *What to Preach*, pp. 166-72.

and occasional response. So what the preacher feels permanently concerning his message will determine the emotional content of the individual sermon. Thus the best emotional preparation for an evangelistic sermon will be made as the preacher reviews his own indebtedness to Christ, and warms his heart once more as he reflects upon the love and loyalty that he owes to his Master in consequence.[7]

A positive mood will further enhance evangelistic sermonic delivery. The preacher should not step into the pulpit with doubts but with certainties. He should leave his critical preparation of the text in his study, standing before his congregation with confidence, as a beacon of divine truth. If he has some questions about his basic biblical passage, he should work them out before he delivers the sermon.

An urgent mood that comes from within and belies artificiality is another part of evangelistic delivery.

The preacher must earn the attention of his hearers each time he steps into the pulpit. Stirring audience interest requires imagination and forethought. An unexpected sentence or comparison of thought will earn attention, as will life-related illustrations gleaned from personal observation. The matter of gaining and sustaining attention is another major difference between a sermon and a lecture.

The evangelistic preacher must be sensitive to the composition of his audience. He should direct his comments not only to the unconverted but to the entire congregation—saints, newborn babes in Christ, the doubters, and the backsliders. Said Breed, "Preach the evangelistic sermon to all classes: preach to the entire congregation. Some will be aroused; some will be convicted; but all will be helped, stimulated, and comforted."[8]

Ideally, the evangelistic preacher must take the time to analyze his audience before, during, and after he speaks to

7. Ozora S. Davis, *Evangelistic Preaching*, pp. 66-67.
8. David R. Breed, *Preparing to Preach*, p. 411..

them. An intimate relationship should develop between the evangelist and his audience if he, under the Spirit of God, hopes to be effective. This was the strong feeling of Finney, who said, "How otherwise can he preach to them? How can he know how to bring forth things new and old, and adapt truth to their case? How can he hunt them out unless he knows where they hide themselves?"[9]

The evangelistic preacher gains several distinct advantages by carefully analyzing his audience. First, a knowledge of the background of the people—their difficulties, trials, and triumphs—will greatly assist him in making his closing appeal more direct. To gain this information, the evangelist must be a keen observer of people. He must know the proper questions to ask the proper people at the proper time. He must gather all this information himself if it is going to be of any help to him. Secondhand knowledge has a way of exposing itself at the most inopportune times. This is one advantage of the pastor's being his own evangelist.

Second, audience analysis will enable the preacher to know which age group he should specifically address. All are to be helped; but if his audience is mainly composed of children, he will want to construct his message differently from the way he would if he were speaking primarily to college students or adults. The occupations of the members of a group are also worth taking into account in seeking to adapt the message to their particular intellectual level.

Third, audience analysis makes it possible for the preacher to anticipate some of the objections that may be raised by honest doubters. As he mingles with people during the week, in their homes and in their places of business, he may learn about some of their difficulties and objections to Christ and the gospel. For example: How do you know the Bible is reliable? Is Jesus Christ God? What about life after death? Isn't

9. Charles G. Finney, *Lectures on Revivals of Religion*, p. 185. For a contemporary discussion of audience analysis and communication theory, see George E. Sweazey's work, *Preaching the Good News*.

the resurrection a hoax? Is Christ the only way? I'm too great a sinner! I could never live for Christ! At least I'm not a hypocrite! These objections, when expressed, can be worked into a series of messages that will speak to the people where they are and lead them to where they ought to be by the grace of God.

Audience analysis during the time the evangelist is on the platform is vital. It enables the preacher to understand the mood of the people and vary his message and thrust accordingly. When the evangelist notices that his audience is restless or antagonistic, he must seek to win their confidence and interest in an honest and frank manner. If they are indifferent or lackadaisical, he must endeavor to arouse and interest them by saying that which is controversial or by challenging their loyalties. If the preacher discovers midway through the sermon that his audience has turned him off, he must be able to change his approach and win them back.

Last, by being a close observer of his audience, the preacher can vary his approach. This should be considered before the sermon. For example, if the preacher knows ahead of time that his audience is mainly non-Christian, he will not begin his message in the normal way by reading his Bible text. Moreover, he will be careful not to use much Christian verbiage and theological dogma that serve only to confuse those who are not familiar with them. He will not want to quote from Christian works or refer to gospel hymns or church history for illustrative material, but rather he will seek to identify completely with the man in the pew so that he can win his confidence and lead him to the cross. He will choose words that do not create barriers between himself and the people with whom he wishes to communicate. Richard R. Caemmerer said, "Style, illustration, directness, must concede to the limited experience of the hearer without condescending!"[10]

Etter offered helpful analysis of the kinds of individuals

10. Richard R. Caemmerer, *Preaching for the Church*, pp. 64-65.

who may be involved in any evangelistic effort. Those kinds of people must become known to the evangelist, and he must try to stimulate them and adapt his preaching to their needs.

The *moralist*—must be convicted of his moral blindness; of the evil of his secret thoughts, intentions, and volitions; of his want of love to God, and the souls of men; of neglect of Bible, prayer, means of grace, self-denials, duties, etc., as well as Christ's command, "Ye must be born again."

The *backslider*—must be reminded of his sad fall, and urged to do his first work over, not by reformation of mere outward conduct, but by true repentance and prayer.

The *unawakened sinner*—must be aroused from his stupor, perhaps by relating some startling incidents or special providences, or recalling some loud calls to him from God through accidents, sickness, or death. . . .

The *convicted sinner*—needs special attention; for many are convicted without repenting. . . . Perhaps he has some idol, or particular sin, which he is not willing to give up; perhaps he has injured someone, and the injuries call for redress and restitution; perhaps he holds a prejudice against someone, feels ill toward some, or is angry and cherishes feelings of resentment. He may be waiting for more conviction, or certain feelings which someone else had before obtaining mercy; perhaps he entertains some errors of doctrine, or wrong notions respecting the thing to be done, or the way of doing it, or may have laid out a plan of his own as to how he expects to be convicted; perhaps he thinks his sins too great to be forgiven, or that he has committed the unpardonable sin, and cannot now be saved. He has many excuses for deferring immediate action, and intrenches himself behind many a refuge of defense. The preacher who would succeed in winning the convicted sinner, must find out his many hiding places, and meet him with arguments such as the case requires. . . .

The *seeking sinner*—must be instructed in the proper method of obtaining salvation; and his difficulties and errors in seeking must be explained and corrected.[11]

11. Etter, pp. 244-45.

The evangelistic preacher will find the following times to be favorable for evangelistically motivating and challenging sermons:

- Advent season (Christmas)
- Lenten season (Easter)
- Passion Week
- Communion observances
- regular church services—morning worship hour, evening evangelistic hour, Wednesday night service
- one or two weeks of concentrated effort in which the pastor or other evangelist comes with an evangelistic thrust
- Sunday school
- a unified service in which the Sunday school and worship hour are combined
- an "unusual occasion"—taking advantage of the courthouse square, the street corner, the park, the resort, the beach, etc.
- the winter months

On the other hand, evangelistic sermons should not be reserved only for special times or occasions. They must be preached when the need for evangelism is evident in the lives of the congregation. The advice of Weatherspoon on this is noteworthy. In concluding his comments about the evangelistic preaching of the apostles, namely Peter, Stephen, and Paul, he said, "The preaching was occasional in the sense that it was not confined to conventional times and places, but was alive to the occasion, having regard to the particular circumstances and using them with tact and insight to obtain a favorable hearing."[12]

## B. Visual Factors in Delivery

We found only one evangelistic writer who had anything to say regarding the visible factors in evangelistic delivery. By

12. Jesse B. Weatherspoon, *Sent Forth to Preach*, p. 124.

visual factors, we simply mean gestures or any other movements that the preacher may engage in while delivering his message.

There are two basic kinds of gestures, the conventional and the autistic:

> Conventional gestures are those which are used to incite strong reactions and to reinforce important ideas. Autistic gestures on the other hand are meaningless gestures which serve to indicate the inner feelings of the speaker rather than to reinforce important ideas. They are normally mere nervous reactions on the part of the speaker.[13]

In the history of classical rhetoric, the elocutionists placed great emphasis on visible factors, insisting that instructions on when and how to gesture be written into the margins of the speaker's manuscript. This mechanical and awkward manner of gesturing was rejected by Finney, who alone recorded any principles for the aspiring evangelist. Hitting hard at elocutionist theory, Finney said:

> But if a man feels his subject fully, he will naturally do it. He will naturally do the thing that elocution laboriously teaches. See any common man in the streets, who is earnest in talking. See with what force he gestures. See a woman or a child, in earnest. How natural. To gesture with their hands is as natural as it is to move their tongue and lips. It is the perfection of eloquence.[14]

On the other hand, the preacher must make certain that his gestures enhance his delivery rather than call attention to it. Nervous gestures can so distract as to render the content of a sermon incomprehensible to the listener. The listener is busy wondering whether the evangelist is going to pull a book out of his inside pocket or take off his glasses when he really gets to the main point of his message. Similarly, imitating the gestures of great evangelists should be avoided. Instead of

13. Perry, p. 186.
14. Finney, p. 196.

141

imitating others, the preacher should strive for that freedom of action that is normal to him as he presents the gospel message.

## C. Audible Factors in Delivery

Audible elements in delivery are crucial. This area of evangelistic delivery involves a basic understanding of phonetics, the science of speech, which unravels the confusion of letters and sounds as well as providing a consistent guide for pronunciation.

There are at least three factors that will determine the audible aspect of the evangelistic delivery. The first is the nature of the audience. The makeup of the audience will largely determine the audible technique of the preacher; that is, whether he will rebuke or encourage, dogmatize or patiently persuade, attack or seek to win over, be apologetic or illustrative.

Second, the audible aspect of sermonic delivery will be determined by the content of the message:

> The man who uses the theme of the judgment will not preach as though he were glad his hearers were going to hell! He will speak with sorrow in his voice, sometimes with tears in his eyes. . . . He will remember an indescribably dramatic scene: Jesus standing outside the wall of Jerusalem, with a broken heart, and exclaiming: "Oh, Jerusalem, Jerusalem, how oft would I have gathered thy children together as a hen gathers her brood under her wings, and ye would not." He will learn from His Master that only broken hearts can heal a broken world.[15]

The third and most important audible factor is the speaker's voice. The effective preacher will take care of his voice and vary his intonations and speed throughout the message. A "preacher tone" should be replaced by a conversational tone. Spurgeon's advice is good: "Shift your accent, move your em-

15. G. Ray Jordan, *You Can Preach*, p. 244.

142

phasis, and avoid sing-song. Vary the tone; use the base some-times, and let the *thunders roll* within; at other times speak as you ought to generally—from the lips, and let your speech be conversational."[16]

There are several key characteristics of effective evangelistic delivery from the standpoint of audible factors. First, the voice of the preacher should be natural and animated. Such audible delivery has been best described by Andrew Blackwood:

> This means enthusiasm in talking things over with the hear-ers. It means using all the charm, the variety, and the win-someness that mark spirited talk at its best. Here stands no dictator sending down pontifical deliverances from some Olympian height, no advocate at the bar defending the Bible as though it were about to be executed. Here speaks a friend, opening up a truth that he has discovered in the Book, and meeting a need that he has found among the people.[17]

There are six factors that will increase one's animation in delivery:

> (1) an intense belief in one's subject, (2) a confidence in one's ability to present one's subject, (3) an eagerness to address that particular audience, (4) a knowledge of the opening sentences of the message, (5) a fervent desire to aid one's listeners, and (6) the possession of an abundance of material on the subject of the message.[18]

The preacher's voice ought to have intensity without being noisy. The following somewhat humorous comment by Biederwolf is appropriate:

> Noise is no evidence of effectiveness. It's no sign of pro-fundity. Deep waters are silent. To roar like a Bashan bull is no sign you are delivering the goods. A lawyer talks to his

16. Charles Spurgeon, "How to Obtain and Retain the Attention of Our Hearers," in *Eminent Authors on Effective Revival Preaching*, ed. Walter P. Doe, pp. 235-36.
17. Andrew W. Blackwood, *Expository Preaching for Today*, pp. 153-54.
18. Perry, p. 186.

jury and tells them what he wants them to know; a teacher does the same to his students. But some preachers preach as though the particular purpose of their appearance in the pulpit is to paralyze the eardrum. If there is the slightest occasion or even excuse for italics they will stand on their toes, get red in the face, swell up in the neck, pull in their diaphragm and push out their chest and yell as if they were trying to reach the island of Madagascar by wireless telephone that was out of order.[19]

Compassion should be in the voice of the preacher as he delivers his evangelistic address. He should not be judgmental in the tone of his delivery. Rather his words should be vibrant with love as he warns, admonishes, and entreats his hearers to accept the truth of the gospel. The compassionate Christ, who was moved when He saw the multitudes, should ever be before the preacher as he prepares and delivers his address. Kindness is part of being compassionate, or, from another viewpoint, is its fruit. Said Roberts:

> Let your tones of voice, as well as your words, be those of one who feels kindly towards all. When you are tempted to say anything harsh, not only resist the temptation, but use just as affectionate language as propriety will permit. Not pounding, but sunbeams soften the frozen ground to receive the plow.[20]

The voice of empathy will awaken a responsive chord in people's hearts. If the preacher can convey to his audience by his intonation that he has faced many of their temptations, that he, too, has been deeply troubled and that, as a minister of the gospel, he is united with them in their fight against sin and Satan, he will have their confidence and loyalty. Empathy can bridge the gulf that often exists between the pulpit and the pew.

19. William E. Biederwolf, *Evangelism: Its Justification, Its Operation and Its Value*, pp. 77-78.
20. B. T. Roberts, *Fishers of Men*, pp. 135-36.

People have a way of soon discovering whether the preacher has to say something or has something to say. In short, people cannot be fooled about the preacher's sincerity or lack of it. The quality of sincerity will strengthen any preacher's delivery and may well mean the difference between acceptance and rejection. The danger of insincerity in delivery is especially heightened in preachers who have been blessed with natural oratorical gifts.

A fervent voice that vibrates with conviction will enhance a speaker's evangelistic delivery. The congregation can soon detect if the preacher is preaching a warmed-over sermon that has not really gripped him in his study. A fervent voice will be the natural outgrowth of a soul that has been set on fire by the fuel of the Word of God. A careless delivery, not backed by intellectual force, cannot be tolerated. An effective evangelistic delivery will vibrate with the truth derived from mental gymnastics.

### D. Physical Factors in Delivery

The setting of an evangelistic sermon is of crucial importance. By "setting" we mean the physical confines within which the sermon is given.

The auditorium or other meeting place must be properly ventilated at all times during a message. Often an unconcerned janitor or a lackadaisical usher, rather than the preacher, has been the cause of failure in an evangelistic campaign; not enough fresh air was circulated, and the people became restless and drowsy.

In like manner, church structure can be an asset or a liability so far as the persuasiveness of the preacher is concerned. A facility in which the people are close to the speaker rather than far removed because of the length of the sanctuary will make for much better communication between the pulpit and the pew.

Another problem that concerns evangelists is the height of

145

the platform. A platform that is three or four steps higher than the main floor causes those sitting in the front pews to constantly look up. That automatically causes people to become sleepy, in addition to putting an unnecessary strain on their necks and shoulders. An ideal platform height is one or two steps higher than the main floor of the sanctuary, providing the floor slopes toward the platform.

Room temperature, the length of the auditorium, and the height of the platform must all be taken into consideration by the preacher who wishes to make a definite impact on the lives of his people.

### E. MUSICAL FACTORS IN DELIVERY

The importance of music in the evangelistic setting was well summarized by George Sweazey:

> Music is of the utmost importance. It can make or break the services. Church music is not an end in itself—it is a device for producing certain spiritual results; it is an instrument for opening hearts to religious influences; it is a vehicle for taking religious truths into minds; it is a form of religious expression.[21]

Music is an essential part of evangelism. L. R. Scarborough said that it is just as important as preaching in creating an appropriate atmosphere. One can take the spiritual temperature of a congregation by the kind of music it creates. The main purposes of evangelistic singing, declared Autry in his book *Basic Evangelism,* are to prepare the hearts of the people to receive the word of the Lord and to secure a decision. Scarborough listed seven benefits that come from employing good gospel music in an evangelistic service:

> 1. Spiritual songs in soul-winning effort *create an evangelistic atmosphere,* tune and temper the heart as nothing else can do. . . .

21. George E. Sweazey, *Effective Evangelism: The Greatest Work in the World,* pp. 178-79.

2. It *enriches the life of preacher* and people and *brings the power of God* into the hearts of men. . . .
3. It *gives the martial spirit* to the people as they make their marches against sin. . . .
4. It is a *powerful evangel of the Gospel.* . . .
5. Its *spiritual cultural effect is very great.* . . .
6. It *wins souls.* . . .
7. It *unites, cements* and *solidifies fellowship* and marshals the forces of Christ's Kingdom.[22]

The convincing power of music was further expounded by John F. Wilson in his chapter on evangelistic music:

a. The rhythm, harmony and melody will convey the text in an understandable way.
b. The beauty of tone and style of performance will add impact to the content of the message.
c. The enthusiasm of the performer will convince the listener of the authenticity of the experience which he claims to have and of which he is singing. . . .
d. The attractiveness of the performer's personality, his appearance and his apparent joy in Christ will cause the listener to desire the same experience.[23]

Without a doubt, a well-planned music program during an evangelistic meeting can be instrumental in leading an individual to Christ, reminding him of prior commitments or challenging him to a deeper experience and fruitful service.

The place music has had in the history of evangelism is worth noting. "There have been no great revivals," declared Scarborough, "where song has not been regnant."[24] John Wilson's *An Introduction to Church Music* devotes an entire chapter to evangelistic music. In that chapter, Wilson summarized the great evangelistic movements of the past and present, showing how music helped to meet the needs of the people.

22. L. R. Scarborough, *With Christ After the Lost,* p. 118.
23. John Wilson, *An Introduction to Church Music,* p. 55.
24. Scarborough, p. 115.

In the sixteenth century, the Reformation was the center of attention. The great need of the period was to get the Word of God into the hands and hearts of the common people. The restoration of music to the people on a large scale during this time was one of the goals. Luther explained the rationale and reciprocal relationship between the songs, the Word of God, and the people, the purpose being: " 'God might speak directly to them in His Word and . . . they might directly answer Him in their songs. ' "[25]

The great need facing the Wesleyan movement of the eighteenth century was to get people to return to a deeper and more personal relationship with God and "to banish the religious sentimentalism that was prevalent in that day." In response to that need, Charles Wesley took "many of the familiar tunes of the day and set sacred texts to them, so that the people would be attracted by the familiarity of the tunes and convicted by the message of the texts."[26]

The New England revivals of the mid-eighteenth century faced the task of stressing in no uncertain terms the grace of God and a gospel that could reach the heart of every man. To meet this challenging need, Jonathan Edwards introduced the hymns of Isaac Watts. So significant were the results that the meetings were called "singing meetings."[27]

The dawn of the nineteenth century saw the rise of the diversified camp meeting movements. In those camp meetings, the basic need was to reach the uneducated and common folk with the gospel in such a way that they could understand it. Quite appropriately, the "gospel song" was born.

The mid-nineteenth century witnessed the evangelistic campaigns of Charles G. Finney. Finney directed his campaign to reach the man in the street who had no church affiliation. In 1831 the Rev. Joshua Leavitt compiled a unique hymnbook designed to appeal to those who were the primary con-

25. Wilson, p. 56.
26. Ibid.
27. Ibid., p. 57.

cern of Finney. Although the hymnbook came under harsh criticism by church leaders because it employed secular tunes with sacred texts, it was readily accepted by the folk for whom it was intended and the results were phenomenal.

D. L. Moody, during his revival meetings of the late nineteenth century, wrestled with the need to present the personal testimonies of believers to non-Christians in a new and better way. Realizing the power of music, Mr. Moody called Ira D. Sankey, gifted singer and songleader, to join him. Sankey's use of the gospel song and the blessing of God on Sankey's ministry are said to have contributed one half of the success Moody enjoyed.

During the early part of the twentieth century, attention was drawn to the evangelistic efforts of Billy Sunday. The needs facing Sunday were twofold: "To give expression to the emotional upheaval which was caused by the country's transition from a rural to an industrial society; to introduce an 'energetic' type of singing and preaching which would attract and appeal to the unchurched." Much as Moody had done with Ira Sankey, Sunday turned to Homer Rodeheaver for help. Rodeheaver stressed songs of personal testimony, and consequently, a "livelier type of gospel singing was introduced."[28]

At present, Billy Graham is being used by God to reach the masses with the gospel. He and his associates are seeking to "reach a society which is culturally and socially minded; to appeal to the educated as well as the uneducated, to the leaders in governmental, religious and theatrical fields as well as to the laborer." Unlike Moody and Sunday, Graham rose to the occasion by forming a musical team composed of a choir, congregational leader, soloist, and two instrumentalists. Moreover, the music in the Billy Graham meetings is "a balance of hymns of praise and worship, standard gospel songs of personal testimony, and some new expressions of fellowship

28. Ibid., p. 58.

with Christ as penned by contemporary songwriters."[29]

The evangelistic song service is a pivotal part of the evangelistic emphasis. It must never be used as a time filler "until the crowd gets there." It must be thoroughly planned and never routine. The song evangelist ought to be a trained musician.

There are four purposes involved in the evangelistic song service: (1) it provides a medium for congregational testimony; (2) it helps to center the attention of the audience on spiritual things; (3) it provides an opportunity for non-Christians to receive a definite spiritual message and become convicted of sin; and (4) it can be a definite means of attraction, drawing non-Christians to the service and thus attracting them to Christ.[30]

The following is Phil Kerr's simple but workable plan for an effective evangelistic song service:

> Begin with an easily sung gospel song with which everyone is familiar
> This may be followed by a few joyful gospel choruses
> Follow these joyful gospel songs with songs of a more serious nature, concluding with a hymn just before prayer
> Following prayer, use another gospel song or chorus
> Special numbers
> Announcements and offering
> Congregational song or special musical number in keeping with the theme of the sermon which is to be delivered.[31]

The power and importance of evangelistic music cannot be denied. Christian music can be an invaluable aid to those who understand its role in the reaching of lost men and women. Music is not an end in itself, but rather a means to an end. When this understanding becomes blurred, music loses its appeal and becomes subject to harsh and rightful criticism. However, history has given adequate testimony to the fact that music moves men.

29. Ibid.
30. Phil Kerr, *Music in Evangelism,* p. 71.
31. Ibid., pp. 71-72.

## F. Spiritual Factors in Delivery

Prayer is also a vital element in the evangelistic setting. The successful evangelistic preacher will not monopolize the prayer time but will encourage the people in the congregation to pray. Roy Short pointed out several ways in which this can be done:

> Frequent periods of sentence prayers
> Unhurried periods of silent prayer
> Periods of congregational prayer in which the preacher suggests possible objects of petition
> Take a verse of Scripture and offer it corporately as a prayer to God[32]

There is all the difference in the world when trying to do the work of an evangelist between a church in which the preacher does almost all the praying and a church in which the people themselves are given to prayer.

The public reading of Scripture in the evangelistic context is dealt with by only one author, so far as we were able to discover. R. A. Torrey, in his detailed treatise *How to Work for Christ,* devoted an entire chapter to the "Preparation and Delivery of Bible Readings." His basic outline is reproduced here:

I. Different kinds of Bible readings. . . .

1. *The Whole Bible Topical Bible Reading.* By this we mean the Bible reading that takes up some topic and goes through the whole Bible to find its texts for the study of the topic. . . .

2. *The Book Topical Bible Reading.* By this we mean the taking up of a topic as it is treated in a single book in the Bible; for example, the Holy Spirit in John's Gospel, or the Believer's Certainties in the First Epistle of John. . . .

3. *The Chapter Topical Bible Reading.* In this the subject is handled simply as it is found in a single chapter in the Bible; for example, the Freedom of the Believer in Rom.

32. Roy H. Short, *Evangelistic Preaching,* p. 87.

viii; or, the Priceless Possessions of the Believer in Phil. iv. . . .

4. *The General Survey of a Book Bible Reading.* In this form of Bible reading there is a rapid survey of the salient facts or great truths of some book in the Bible.

5. *The General Survey of a Chapter Bible Reading.* This varies from the preceding one, in that a single chapter is considered instead of an entire book.

6. *The Running Commentary Bible Reading.*

7. *The Mutual Help Bible Reading.*

II. The choice of subjects. . . .

1. *There are some great subjects that every pastor and teacher and evangelist should take up, such as the following:*

(1) The Power of the Blood of Christ.
(2) The Power of the Word of God.
(3) The Power of the Holy Spirit.
(4) The Power of Prayer.
(5) How to Pray Effectually.
(6) Justification.
(7) The New Birth.
(8) Sanctification.
(9) God's Plan for Every Believer's Life.
(10) Assurance.
(11) Faith.
(12) Repentance.
(13) Love.
(14) Thanksgiving.
(15) Worship.
(16) Future Destiny of Believers.
(17) Future Destiny of Impenitent Sinners.
(18) The Second Coming of Christ.
(19) Fulfilled Prophecies.

2. *Go through Bible Text Books and Concordances, noting subjects for Bible Readings.*

3. *Get suggestions from suggestive books of Bible Readings.* . . .

4. *Keep a blank book and note down such subjects as occur to you from time to time.*

5. *Get your subject for the meeting immediately in hand by prayer.*

III. The getting together of material for Bible readings. . . .

1. *Look up in the Concordance the passages having the word or synonymous words in it. . . .*

2. *Look up the subject and related subjects in your topical text book. . . .*

3. *Look up the subject and related subjects in the book, "What the Bible Teaches."*

4. *In your general Bible study be always on the watch for passages bearing on the subjects upon which you intend to teach. . . .*

5. *Put on your thinking cap and see if you cannot call to mind passages on the subject in hand.*

IV. The selection and arrangement of material.

1. *Having gotten your material together, see what you can dispense with, and strike it out at once.* The following four points will be helpful in the exclusion of material:

(1) Substantially the same material in different forms.

(2) Comparatively unimportant material.

(3) Material not adapted to the needs of the congregation for which you are preparing.

(4) Material about which you are uncertain.

2. *Form your principal divisions and arrange your remaining material under them. . . .*

3. *Get your divisions in the best possible order, and the subdivisions under them also in the best order.* The following suggestions will help in this:

(1) Bring together points that naturally go together.

(2) As far as possible have each point lead naturally up to the next point.

(3) When possible, have a climax of thought with the strongest point last.

(4) Put the points that lead naturally to decision and action last.

V. The delivery of the Bible reading.

1. *Sometimes give the passages out to others to read.*
(1) Write them out on slips of paper and hand them out. . . .
(2) Call the passages off, and have those who take them call them out after you. . . .

2. *Oftentimes read the passages yourself.*[33]

The final aspect of the spiritual setting is worship. Again, only Short made any helpful contribution regarding worship and evangelism. Commenting on the accepted practice that the morning service is for worship and the evening service for evangelism, he said, "The truth is that there should be no antithesis between worship and evangelism. True worship helps to accomplish the work of evangelism and true evangelism should surely be worshipful."[34]

## G. Delivery Methods

### 1. Extemporaneous Delivery

Almost without exception among the writers in the fields of homiletic and evangelistic theory, extemporaneous delivery is the preferred method of presenting evangelistic sermons. John Broadus defined such speech in the following manner: "Extemporaneous speaking is applied to cases in which there has been preparation of the thought, but the language is left to be suggested at the moment."[35] Thus, to preach extemporaneously does not mean to preach unprepared. The extemporaneous preacher more than any other needs to be saturated with the facts and features of the biblical text. His illustrations and analogies must not merely be on paper but en-

33. Reuben A. Torrey, *How to Work for Christ*, pp. 339-43.
34. Short, pp. 42-43.
35. John A. Broadus, "Extemporaneous Speaking," in Doe, p. 210.

grained in his mind. His content should be just as full as that of the manuscript preacher.

The only difference between the extemporaneous preacher and the manuscript preacher comes when the content of the message is clothed with language. The manuscript preacher clothes his content with language before he delivers it, whereas the extemporaneous preacher waits until he stands before his audience with a full heart and mind. At such times the Holy Spirit has a special relationship to the mind of the speaker. The Holy Spirit guides and directs the speaker's mind as he relates the truth that he has carefully studied beforehand. Someone has said that a preacher should prepare his sermon as if there were no such person as the Holy Spirit and then deliver his sermon as if there were no one but the Holy Spirit.

The advantages of preaching extemporaneously were stated concisely by Broadus:

1. In preparation, this method accustoms one to think more rapidly and with less dependence on external helps, than if he habitually wrote in full.

2. It also enables a man to spend his strength chiefly upon the more difficult or more important parts of the subject.

3. In general, this method saves time for general improvement and other pastoral work, after he has gained facility and self-reliance in preparation.

4. In the act of delivery, the extemporaneous speaker has immense advantages. With far greater ease and effectiveness he can turn to account ideas which occur at the time.

5. The whole mass of prepared material becomes brightened, warmed, and sometimes transfigured by this inspiration of delivery. . . .

6. The preacher can watch the effect as he proceeds, and purposely alter the forms of expression, as well as the manner of delivery, according to his own feelings and that of the audience.

7. It leads to more dependence upon the Holy Spirit, and prayer for his help in preaching.
8. As to the delivery itself, it is only in extemporaneous speaking, of one or another variety, that this can ever be perfectly natural, and achieve the highest effect.
9. With the masses it is the more preferred method.[36]

Successful extemporaneous delivery is possible only if the preacher is the master of his subject. Such mastery presupposes diligent and careful study. The preacher must be a master not only of his subject but also of the English language. He must have a large vocabulary and an abundant interest in words. Finally, he must have the capacity to digest readily that which he reads and studies. His memory must be keen, able to recall key ideas that are relevant to the sermon he is delivering.

Why extemporaneous preaching is the preferred method of delivering evangelistic sermons was expressed by Finney:

1. No set of men can stand the labor of writing sermons and doing all the preaching which will be requisite.
2. Written preaching is not calculated to produce the requisite effect. Such preaching does not present truth in the right shape.
3. It is impossible for a man who writes his sermons to arrange his matter, and turn and choose his thoughts, so as to produce the same effect as when he addresses the people directly, and makes them feel that he means them.[37]

There are, on the other hand, serious disadvantages to extemporaneous preaching. As listed by Broadus, they are as follows:

1. There may be a tendency to neglect preparation, after one has gained facility in this way.
2. There is difficulty in fixing the mind upon the work of preparation without writing in full.

36. Ibid., pp. 210-12.
37. Finney, p. 200.

3. The extemporizer cannot quote so largely as the reader, from Scripture, or from the writings of others.
4. The style of an extemporaneous sermon is apt to be less condensed and less finished, than if it were written out and read.
5. The success of an extemporaneous sermon is largely dependent upon the preacher's feelings at the time of delivery, and upon the circumstances; so that he is liable to decided failure.
6. If the sermon is to be used again, and has not been written out in full, it requires some renewed preparation.
7. Still another disadvantage is its tendency to prevent one's forming the habit of writing.[38]

We believe Broadus was correct when he concluded that these disadvantages can be overcome through diligent work. On the other hand, the disadvantages inherent in the manuscript method of delivery (pp. 177-79) can only be diminished; they can never be completely removed.

The objection raised by promoters of the manuscript method that extemporaneous preaching does away with thinking was rightfully disagreed with by Finney:

The man who writes least may, if he pleases, *think most*, and will say what he does think in a manner that will be better understood than if it were written; and that, just in the proportion that he lays aside the labor of writing, his body will be left free to exercise, and his mind to vigorous and consecutive thought.[39]

For positive suggestions for developing evangelistic extemporaneous delivery, James M. Hoppin is helpful:

1. Train yourself to think without writing.
2. Think through the subject beforehand.
3. Prepare beforehand, either mentally or on paper, the actual wording of your main proposition and the prin-

38. Broadus, pp. 212-14.
39. Finney, pp. 201-2.

cipal divisions, and perhaps some of the most important passages.

4. Cultivate the faculty of free and correct expression.
5. Make a beginning at once.
6. Do not choose too easy or familiar subjects.
7. Look above the opinion of men upon your preaching.
8. Mingle the written and extemporaneous methods. Let one preach a written sermon in the morning, and an extemporaneous one in the afternoon, and let him never think of writing out his weekly lectures or other public addresses.
9. Cultivate oratorical delivery. . . . The extemporizer should acquire a clear, distinct articulation, rising and falling naturally with the thought, varied and yet even; neat and yet capable of feeling, and of vehement, rending force; and above all, free from tones of earthly passion, and breathing pure, holy spiritual emotions.[40]

## 2. READING FROM MANUSCRIPT

Almost all the writers in Doe's work commended the extemporaneous method, and they spent an equal amount of space criticizing the manuscript method. Finney said, "Let your sermons be written with a high degree of literary finish."[41] Porter pointed out that Jesus and the apostles did not use manuscripts. They spoke from full hearts and keen minds that had digested the verities of the Word of God. Porter also made the interesting point, "Reading sermons is a modern invention, owing its origin to political jealousy. With jealousy it should have passed away into everlasting disuse."[42]

According to Broadus, there are four inherent advantages in using the manuscript method of delivery: (1) ease in fixing the mind on the subject; (2) completeness of preparation; (3) excellence of style; and (4) ease in delivery.[43]

40. James M. Hoppin, "Extempore Sermons," in Doe, pp. 225-27.
41. Charles G. Finney, "Preaching So As to Convert Nobody," in Doe, p. 52.
42. James Porter, *Revivals of Religion*, p. 90.
43. Broadus, p. 208.

On the other hand, the disadvantages of the manuscript method are many and varied:

- One becomes so dependent on his manuscript that his delivery is unnatural.
- The written manuscript may be superficial and hurried.
- The written manuscript consumes too much time in mere mechanical effort.
- The written manuscript compels the preacher to follow out the plan, although subsequent thought may show that another plan would be better.
- Using a written manuscript deprives the preacher of the mental quickening produced by the exciting presence and sympathy of an attentive congregation.
- The written manuscript makes any attempt at animation look clumsy and forced.
- The tonal quality of the voice may tend to grow monotonous or have a forced variety.
- The preacher's gestures are inhibited and nearly always unnatural.
- Eye contact with the audience is impossible.
- To read from a manuscript means that repetition of key thoughts and concepts throughout the sermon is lost.
- To read from a manuscript makes it impossible for the preacher to analyze his audience. He will not be able to notice whether he is communicating with them. Audience feedback will be nil. The extemporaneous preacher, on the other hand, is able to detect whether the audience really understands him. If he sees they do not, he can rephrase his thoughts, change his terminology, or insert an illustration that will bring the audience back to him.
- Also, in attempting now and then to look up from the manuscript, the preacher may lose his place or train of thought and get frustrated and ultimately confused, to the utter dismay and dissatisfaction of his audience.

- A manuscript raises communication barriers immediately—the people immediately assume that the message is going to be dry and uninteresting. Moreover, it may indicate an air of artificiality.
- To read from a manuscript is injurious to the voice.
- The habit of reading from a manuscript may cause the preacher great embarrassment when circumstances call for him to be without notes.

In short, reading from a manuscript destroys the total effect of the evangelistic sermon. Porter concluded:

> Reading deranges the whole, so that no one speaks naturally. There is power, also, in gesture, but reading destroys it. In fact, it mars the whole performance. The heart is comparatively stupefied, the hands tied, the feet fettered, the body often transfixed, and every expression of the countenance perverted.[44]

Henry Ward Beecher added this criticism: "This intolerable bondage let every minister avoid—let him not be shut up in such narrow limits, having no more power than a canal whose channel is dug for it."[45]

Still, there are those who, despite the disadvantages, will choose manuscript preaching simply because they cannot force themselves to extemporize or have no inclination toward it. Such evangelists should read their manuscripts so thoroughly and repeatedly just before entering the pulpit that the sermons can be delivered freely, without confining the eyes to anything more than an occasional and slight glance at the beginning of each successive paragraph. The manuscript method should be used only as running shoes to speed the spiritual progress of the message, not as crutches to impede it. In some cases the preacher may want to write out his sermons in their entirety and then form bare outlines that he can take

44. Porter, p. 89.
45. Henry Ward Beecher, "The Ministerial Work," in Doe, p. 94.

with him into the pulpit. That would be a happy medium between the extemporaneous and manuscript methods, and that method may be of value to the aspiring evangelist in the beginning stages of his ministry.

# VII

## *Summary of Principles for Power in Evangelistic Preaching*

THE FOLLOWING PRINCIPLES are drawn from the preceding chapters.  If implemented, these principles can enable one to preach evangelistically with power, purpose, and the anointing of the Spirit of God.

### A. INVENTION: THE PREPARATION OF AN EVANGELISTIC MESSAGE

The evangelistic preacher must be prepared to spend long hours of study in preparation for his sermon.  He should not substitute eloquence for Bible content.  He must desire intellectual activity, for, as Roland Leavell observed, "Evangelists today must *know* something as well as *feel* something.  God never puts a premium on an empty brain just because one has a full heart."[1]

The evangelistic preacher must begin his sermon preparation with the Bible.  He must not begin with an idea and then find biblical support.  He must begin with the biblical text and develop that text through observation, interpretation, and application. Exegesis rather than eisegesis must be his method.

The evangelistic preacher must preach from the whole Bible—both Old and New Testaments.  He must avoid personal hobbyhorse texts and preach the whole counsel of God.

1.  Roland Leavell, *Evangelism: Christ's Imperative Commission*, p. 104.

The evangelistic preacher should be concerned primarily with preaching doctrine relevantly and definitively to his hearers. Doctrine must precede duty. Creed must come before conduct. Doctrine, together with the convicting power of the Holy Spirit, provides a sound basis for a genuine conversion.

The evangelistic preacher must interpret the text before he applies it. He must seek to get to the meaning intended by the author of the particular Bible passage that he is preparing to use.

The evangelistic preacher must derive his subject from the preaching portion. He must not impose a subject upon a text. His theme must be a particular aspect of his subject, which is based on the biblical text.

The evangelistic preacher must give much thought to the selection of a title for his sermon. The title must arrest attention and relate to the theme the preacher has chosen. A sensational title or a title that does not tie in with the biblical content of the message is deceptive and unethical.

The evangelistic preacher must not only expound the biblical text; he must also apply it to the everyday lives of the listeners. Relevant applications, directed in love to the men and women in the pews, cause those men and women to examine their lives in light of the preaching text. Applications must be thought through and be deeply significant, and they must never be mundane.

The evangelistic preacher must try to prepare a sermon that is logical, rational, and factual. It should appeal to the thinking man in the pew.

The evangelistic preacher must select appropriate illustrations that illuminate rather than obliterate the main point of the message. Illustrations must be kept in balance. An evangelistic message must not be a series of stories and anecdotes, but an exposition of biblical content.

The evangelistic preacher should give serious consideration

to developing a long-range preaching program. Such disciplined preparation will not only stimulate the preacher's mind, but it will also enable him to preach the whole gospel of God evangelistically.

The evangelistic preacher must be a careful observer of the particular setting in which he is ministering. He must be sensitive not only to the structural aspects of the building, but also to his listeners' nonverbal actions and reactions. Audience analysis must be part of his preparation before, after, and during his presentation. The evangelistic preacher should be knowledgeable about appropriate evangelistic music. It would be well for him to tie in the music of a campaign with the main point of his messages.

### B. Arrangement: The Organization of an Evangelistic Message

The evangelistic preacher must spend ample time organizing his gathered materials into a rational and coherent structural framework.

The evangelistic preacher's organization must begin with the biblical preaching portion. In so doing, he is able to expound and apply biblical truth in a systematic progression of thought.

The evangelistic preacher must select a proposition that is drawn from the sermonic theme and is relevant to life. It is at this point that many evangelistic sermons fail. An evangelistic sermon without a clear proposition contributes to incoherency of thought and a topical rather than an expository approach.

The evangelistic preacher should follow the transitional process as outlined on pages 96-99. That will enable him to move smoothly and consistently from his introduction and explanation to his main divisions. Moreover, it will mean that all main divisions will logically support his proposition.

The evangelistic preacher must draw his main points from the preaching text. Main points should not be drawn from texts or parts of texts that are questionable so far as the Greek and Hebrew manuscripts are concerned.

The evangelistic preacher should develop his main divisions by adding subdivisions drawn from the preaching portion. With the subpoints clarifying any given main division, an illustration and a subpoint application should be included.

The evangelistic preacher should formulate an introduction only after he has completed his sermon body (proposition, transitional process, main divisions, and subdivisions).

The evangelistic preacher should prepare and plan out his conclusion in as much detail as the main body of his message. The conclusion must not be detached from the message emphasis or become a second sermon.

The evangelistic preacher must avoid manipulating people in his invitation. The invitation must be related to the message's emphasis and appeal to the intellects, emotions, and volitions of the people in the pews.

The evangelistic preacher should become thoroughly acquainted with the many possible variations of the evangelistic invitation (pp. 109-13). Such knowledge enables him to avoid an invitatory rut and also helps him to know what new approach is available if the situation demands one.

The evangelistic preacher must rely completely on the Holy Spirit when issuing an invitation. It is the Holy Spirit who convicts and compels men to repent of their sins.

## C. Style: The Locution of an Evangelistic Message

The evangelistic preacher must seek to develop a lucid and articulate style that is understandable to the average man in the pew. He must mean what he says and say what he means.

The evangelistic preacher must refrain from using poor English and being verbose.

The evangelistic preacher must repeat key words and thoughts for emphasis throughout his message. The main divisions especially should be repeated.

The evangelistic preacher must cultivate a vocabulary that enables his hearers to visualize what he is saying to them. He must use descriptive language that turns listeners' ears into "eyes."

The evangelistic preacher must develop a style that is natural, simple, life-related, clear, personal, educational, emphatic, animated, moral, biblical, direct, and urgent.

### D. DELIVERY: THE PRESENTATION OF AN EVANGELISTIC MESSAGE

The evangelistic preacher must try to develop a persuasive delivery that involves logos (facts), pathos (emotions), and ethos (ethics).

The evangelistic preacher must become aware of the motives that move men (pp. 132-34).

The evangelistic preacher must not avoid emotion in his preaching. One who grapples deeply with the text cannot help but feel strongly about the message. A heart that is genuinely stirred will manifest emotion. Pseudoemotionalism (emotion for the sake of emotion), however, should not find its way into evangelistic preaching.

The evangelistic preacher should employ gestures meaningfully and naturally in such a way that they enhance rather than detract from the biblical emphasis of his sermon.

The evangelistic preacher will avoid what is commonly known as a "preacher's tone." He will strive to develop a conversational tone, speaking *to* his audience rather than *at* them.

The evangelistic preacher will speak extemporaneously. He will not tie himself down to a manuscript, which inhibits his freedom of thought, his gestures, and his observation of audience feedback.

The words of Henry C. Fish provide a fitting summation:

> A sermon may be constructed after the best models; it may conform to all the rules of homiletics; the text may be suitable and fruitful; the plan may be faultless; the execution

166

may discover genius and judgment; there may be accurate analysis and strong reasoning; proof and motive; solidarity and beauty; logic and passion; argument direct and indirect; perspicuity, purity, correctness, propriety, precision; description, antithesis, metaphor, allegory, comparison; motives from goodness, motives from happiness, motives from self-love; appeals to the sense of the beautiful, the sense of right, to the affections, the passions, the emotions;—a sermon may be all this, and yet that very sermon, even though it fell from the lips of a prince of pulpit oratory, were as powerless in the renewal of a soul as in raising the dead, if unaccompanied by the omnipotent energy of the Holy Ghost.[2]

2.  Henry C. Fish, *Handbook of Revivals,* p. 281.

# Conclusion

DR. FARIS D. WHITESELL lamented more than thirty years ago, "Too much so-called evangelistic preaching has been shallow, partisan, and emotional without much thought content."[1] Today, as then, the great need of the hour is exposition in evangelism. The evangelistic preacher must have something to say to a dying world. The Word of God must be as a fire burning in his soul. His mind and heart must be filled with the biblical text. He must work in the text with toil and tears, allowing it to take hold in his own experience and then through the power of the Holy Spirit become an agent in changing the lives of searching people. He must work with the original languages of the text (if at all possible), seek to appreciate the history and culture of the biblical writer, and try to respond to the original author's intention with cogent applications that make their mark. Only then will the evangelistic sermon be biblically accurate, intellectually stimulating, relevant, and spiritually transforming.

Peter's sermon on the day of Pentecost was an evangelistic masterpiece. Its aim was to *convince* the minds of his listeners of the credibility of Christ (Acts 2:36); to *convict* the consciences of the people in his congregation concerning the claims of Christ (Acts 2:37-38); and to *communicate* the eternal hope of the gospel that centers totally in the Person of Christ (Acts 2:39).

Not only will such a commitment to evangelistic exposition enrich the evangelist, but the people to whom he ministers

1. Faris D. Whitesell, *Evangelistic Preaching and the Old Testament*, p. 34.

will become acquainted with the Word. The church has enough biblical illiterates! What people need to know better is not this world but rather the world that is to come as seen through the lens of holy Scripture. Exposition in evangelism will enable people to discriminate between religious fads and real truth that is eternal. The result is that souls will be saved and believers will be built up in the faith.

The great evangelistic preacher F. B. Meyer understood the awe and responsibility with which the biblical expositor comes to his task:

> The expositor of the Bible is . . . in the line of a great succession. The Reformers, the Puritans, the pastors of the Pilgrim fathers were essentially expositors. They did not announce their own particular opinions, which might be a matter of private interpretation or doubtful disposition; but taking their stand on scripture, drove home their message with irresistable effect with, "Thus saith the Lord."[2]

For the evangelist of today, such a conviction will bring personal renewal, revitalization to the evangelistic message, and revival to the church. Evangelistic preaching can be authentic, biblical, and powerful.

> Send forth thy heralds, Lord, to call
> The thoughtless young, the hardened old,
> A scattered, homeless flock, till all
> Be gathered to thy peaceful fold.
> WILLIAM CULLEN BRYANT

---

2. F. B. Meyer, *Expository Preaching Plans and Methods*, p. 60.

## The Rhetorical Emphases of Great Evangelistic Preachers

| Periods of Church History | Preacher | Invention | Arrangement | Style | Memory | Delivery |
|---|---|---|---|---|---|---|
| The Patristic Age | Chrysostom | x | | x | | x |
| The Early Medieval Period | | | | | | |
| The Central Medieval Age | Bernard of Clairvaux | | x | x | | x |
| | Dominic | x | | | | |
| | Anthony of Padua | x | x | | | |
| | Berthold of Regensburg | x | x | | | x |
| The Renaissance and Late Medieval Age | John Tauler of Strasburg | x | x | | | |
| | Gerhard Groot | x | | | | |
| | John Geiler of Kaisersberg | x | x | | | |
| The Reformation Period | Hugh Latimer | x | | x | | x |
| | William Farel | | | | | x |
| | John Bradford | x | x | | | |
| The Early Modern Period | Richard Baxter | | x | x | | x |
| | Paolo Segneri | x | x | | | x |
| | John Bunyan | | x | x | | |
| | Jacques Bridaine | | | | | x |
| | John Wesley | x | x | x | | x |
| | Gilbert Tennent | x | | x | | |
| | George Whitefield | | | x | | x |

| Periods of Church History | Preacher | Invention | Arrangement | Style | Memory | Delivery |
|---|---|---|---|---|---|---|
| *The Late Modern Period* | Johann Caspar Lavater | x | x | | | x |
| | Rowland Hill | x | x | | | x |
| | Richard Moore | x | | | | |
| | Christmas Evans | x | x | x | | x |
| | Leigh Richmond | x | | | x | |
| | Klaus Harms | | x | | | |
| | Jabez Bunting | | | | | |
| | John Angell James | x | x | | | x |
| | Nathaniel Taylor | x | x | | | x |
| | Charles G. Finney | x | x | x | | x |
| | Ludwig Hofacker | x | | | | x |
| | Charles Spurgeon | x | x | x | | x |
| | Dwight L. Moody | x | x | x | | x |
| | Frederick B. Meyer | x | | x | | x |
| | Samuel P. Jones | x | | x | | x |
| *The Twentieth Century* | Amzi C. Dixon | | x | | | x |
| | Reuben A. Torrey | | x | | | x |
| | B. Fay Mills | x | x | | | x |
| | J. Wilbur Chapman | | x | x | | x |
| | William A. (Billy) Sunday | x | | | | x |
| | Walter A. Maier | x | | x | | x |
| | William F. (Billy) Graham | x | x | x | | x |

# APPENDIX B

## *Chronological Listing of Notable Evangelistic Preachers*

*The Patristic Age* (A.D. 70-430)
Irenaeus
Chrysostom (347?-407)
Hilary (?-368) ·
Augustine (354-430)
*The Early Medieval Period* (430-1095)
St. Patrick (372?-461?)
St. Ninian (b. 432?)
Columban (540?-615?)
Gallus (550?-640)
Wilfrid (634-709)
Winfrid (680-755)
Ansgar (801-65)
*The Central Medieval Age* (1095-1300)
Bernard of Clairvaux (1091-1153)
Dominic (1170-1221)
Anthony of Padua (1195?-1231)
Berthold of Regensburg (1220?-72?)
*The Renaissance & Late Medieval Age* (1300-1500)
John Tauler of Strasburg (1290-1361)
Gerhard Groot (1349-84)
John Geiler of Kaisersberg (1445-1510)

*The Reformation Period* (1500-72)
   Hugh Latimer (1485?-1555)
   William Farel (1489-1565)
   John Bradford (1510?-55)
   Bernard Gilpin (1517-83)
*The Early Modern Period* (1572-1789)
   John Livingstone (1603-72)
   Richard Baxter (1615-91)
   Vavasor Powell (1617-71)
   Paolo Segneri (1624-94)
   John Bunyan (1628-88)
   Theodore J. Frelinghuysen (1691-1748)
   Jacques Bridaine (1701-67)
   John Wesley (1703-91)
   Gilbert Tennent (1703-64)
   Daniel Marshall (1706-79)
   Samuel Blair (1712-51)
   Daniel Rowlands (1713-90)
   George Whitefield (1714-70)
   William Williams (1717-91)
   James McGready (1758-1817)
*The Late Modern Period* (1789-1900)
   Johann Caspar Lavater (1741-1801)
   Rowland Hill (1744-1833)
   Richard Moore (1762-1841)
   Robert Roberts (1762-1802)
   Christmas Evans (1766-1838)
   William Jay (1769-1853)
   Leigh Richmond (1772-1827)
   Klaus Harms (1778-1855)
   Jabez Bunting (1779-1858)
   John Angell James (1785-1859)
   Nathaniel Taylor (1786-1858)
   Charles G. Finney (1792-1875)
   Ludwig Hofacker (1798-1828)

Edward N. Kirk  (1802-74)
Alassandro Gavazzi  (1809-91)
Robert McCheyne  (1813-43)
Henry W. Beecher  (1813-87)
Giovanni Pietro Meille  (1817-87)
Andrew K. Boyd  (1825-99)
Joseph Parker  (1830-1902)
Charles Spurgeon  (1834-92)
Dwight L. Moody  (1837-99)
Frederick B. Meyer  (1847-1929)
Samuel P. Jones  (1847-1906)
*The Twentieth Century*  (1900-Present)
Amzi C. Dixon  (1854-1925)
Reuben A. Torrey  (1856-1928)
W. Y. Fullerton  (1857-1932)
B. Fay Mills  (1857-1916)
J. Wilbur Chapman  (1859-1918)
Rodney "Gypsy" Smith  (1860-1947)
William A. (Billy) Sunday  (1863-1935)
William E. Biederwolf  (1867-1939)
Walter A. Maier  (1893-1950)
William F. (Billy) Graham  (b. 1918)

# APPENDIX C

# *Evangelistic Sermon Starters*

### LIFE AT THE CROSSROADS

And we set out from Horeb, and went through all that great and terrible wilderness which you saw, on the way to the hill country of the Amorites, as the LORD our God commanded us; and we came to Kadesh-barnea (Deut. 1:19, RSV).

It has been said that Kadesh-barnea was the most important biblical locality during the years covered by the book of Deuteronomy. The name means "holy place."

Kadesh-barnea could be called the crossroads of the Old Testament. It was from Kadesh-barnea that the spies went into the promised land to make a survey prior to the invasion by God's people. When the spies returned from their mission, ten of the twelve said that it was impossible to go forward because of insurmountable hindrances. Two of the twelve, Caleb and Joshua, formed God's minority and declared that although there were giants ahead, God was also there. But the majority decision held, and a nation turned back from Kadesh-barnea to die in the desert.

Decision determines destiny. Big doors swing on small hinges. You may be standing now at a modern Kadesh-barnea. Your decision at Kadesh-barnea will determine your location—either in the desert or in the promised land.

*Do not trifle at the crossroads.* Life consists of the sum of our decisions. Victory comes when the wavering mind sets forth in one direction. We cannot afford to trifle with the choice of a life's mate, the choice of an occoupation, or especially with the choice of a Savior from sin for eternity. An individual life, career, family, or nation's welfare may be hanging in the balance. Eternity may be at stake. Do not trifle.

*Others will be influenced by your decision at the crossroad.* Only Caleb and Joshua were permitted to enter the promised land (Deut. 1:34-37). No one lives to himself. Little feet may be following in large footprints. Achan's covetousness (Josh. 7) meant that his family suffered as well as Achan himself. The prodigal returned (Luke 15:11-32), but what happened to all the friends in the far country whom he by his example and encouragement had drawn into sin?

*Decisions should only be made after God has been taken into consideration.* Many of their friends discouraged them (Deut. 1:28), but Caleb and Joshua remembered that the Lord would go with them and fight for them (Deut. 1:30). One with God is a majority. How great is your God? Two of the great words of Scripture are found at the beginning of Ephesians 2:4, "But God." He makes all the difference. Do not go forward if He is not with you. Do not hesitate to go if you are confident that He is on your side. Beware of the foolishness of the rich fool (Luke 12:16-21) who left God out of his thinking, his planning, and his philosophy of life.

It is not wise to delay at an intersection. A decision must be made at the crossroad. A very short time elapses between the change of the traffic light from red to green and the blowing of the automobile horn behind you, signaling you to get going. Convictions get weaker, desires dwindle, and forces of opposition gather while you delay. Now is the accepted time. Lingering Lot (Gen. 19:16) lost. Many have discovered that they have lost as they have lingered. It is Satan who will try to convince you that there is plenty of time.

What if God were to take you in your lingering? To be almost persuaded is to be almost saved. To be almost saved is to be completely lost.

## SILENCE THE SHEEP
### (1 Sam. 15:10-23)

The verse that forms the center of this meditation poses one of the many embarrassing questions in the Bible: "And Samuel said, 'What meaneth then this bleating of the sheep in mine ears, and the lowing of the oxen which I hear?' " (1 Sam. 15:14).

As God's people journeyed from the land of bondage in Egypt to the land of blessing in Canaan, they faced strong opposition from the Amalekites. God was very much aware of this opposition; He always cares for His own and knows of their hardship as well as their happiness. A command was given to destroy the nation that had oppressed God's chosen people: "Now go and smite Amalek, and utterly destroy all that they have, and spare them not; but slay both man and woman, infant and suckling, ox and sheep, camel and ass" (1 Sam. 15:3).

The responsibility for carrying out those instructions was given to Saul. He gathered 200,000 footmen and 10,000 men of Judah and proceeded toward the execution of his task. But instead of doing exactly as he had been commanded by God to do, Saul put his own interpretation upon God's command and spared Agag and the best of the animals. That failure to obey God's command prompted God to take steps to relieve Saul of his leadership (1 Sam. 15:10-12).

When Samuel, the prophet of God, confronted Saul, Saul tried to lie and thus attempted to cover up his disobedience (1 Sam. 15:13). Samuel then unmasked the disobedience and falsehood by calling attention to the bleating of the sheep. Their bleating was indisputable evidence that Saul had not followed the instructions of God. If the sheep had been silent, Saul might have delayed the uncovering of his disobedience. Experience seems to show, however, that the sheep always bleat at the wrong time.

179

*God demands complete obedience* (1 Sam. 15:9). Saul decided to keep King Agag for vanity's sake and the animals for reason's sake. He destroyed that which was vile. That was his wrong interpretation of God's command. His statement that he disobeyed so that he could sacrifice to God did not absolve him from responsibility. The end does not justify the means. "To obey is better than sacrifice" (1 Sam. 15:22*b*). Moral conduct is more important than ceremonial form and practice. "Rebellion is as the sin of witchcraft, and stubbornness is as iniquity" (1 Sam. 15:23*a*). Partial obedience to God brought rejection of Saul as a leader.

*God detects disobedience* (1 Sam. 15:10-11). The declarations of Scripture emphasize this fact: "Behold, ye have sinned against the Lord: and be sure your sin will find you out" (Num. 32:23). God's holy nature and the witness of experience also assure us of God's detection of disobedience. This truth should speak to us of the futility of sinful pretense. God knows our real nature.

*God desires more than conviction of disobedience. Saul said more often than any other Bible character, "I have sinned"* (1 Sam. 15:24, 30). Although he declared it, however, he did nothing to rectify the situation. Saul was evidently not troubled that he had disobeyed God, but instead he was troubled lest he should lose his leadership. After he realized that his sin was public knowledge, he asked Samuel for forgiveness (1 Sam. 15:25). He had confessed his sin under pressure and then sought to gain approval from man but not God. Saul's day of grace had expired, and although he pleaded for a reprieve, there was none to receive. There is a limit to the patience of God.

Saul struggled with circumstances and lost. He was a man of great potential, but it crumbled on his day of decision. Disobedience to God can be rectified through following 1 John 1:9: "If we confess our sins, he is faithful and just to forgive us our sins, and to cleanse us from all unrighteousness."

## SATISFACTION GUARANTEED
### (Isa. 55:1-13)

When the American Bible Society conducted a survey to discover people's fifteen favorite chapters of the Bible, it found that Isaiah 55 was one of those top fifteen. The style of the chapter is such that one is in the very stardust of Scripture when reading it. Its emphasis upon guaranteed satisfaction answers a common longing of the human heart. Education and civilization do not produce satisfied people. The more we have and know, the more we want to have and know.

The people to whom Isaiah 55 was first directed were displaced, disillusioned, disheartened, and despairing. They were going through life without hope. They had suffered hardships, heartaches, and hopelessness. That chapter, with its invitation to come to God for satisfaction, must have blessed their hearts as a cool breeze after a hot day refreshes the body. Clarence McCartney referred to *come* as God's favorite word. God has invited people to come to Him for safety, sight, service, and satisfaction. God's offer of satisfaction is unique.

*God's offer of satisfaction is unique in its price.* "Come ye to the waters, and he that hath no money; come ye, buy, and eat . . . without money and without price" (Isa. 55:1). Men and women are invited to buy wine (gladness) and milk (nourishment). The implication of this statement pertaining to price might be that the items are beyond the reach of money. The implication could also be that the One selling the items does not need the money. Another implication might be that the price has already been paid. When God has made such an offer, we wonder with the prophet why people spend money for that which is not nourishing and labor for that which does not really satisfy.

*God's offer of satisfaction is unique in its proposition.* The invitation is made without restriction. Man's part is summarized by six simple words of action. Three of those words

181

are found in verse 1: come, buy, and eat. Two of the verbs are found in verse 7. Those words imply immediacy, initiative, and action. God's part involves the confirmation of the offer through Christ (Isa. 55:4), the declaration of the offer by God Himself (Isa. 55:8-9), and the recording of the offer in God's infallible Word (Isa. 55:11).

*God's offer of satisfaction is unique in its provision.* The provision is made for man's going forth with joy and peace (Isa. 55:12). The sharp, piercing, pain-causing thorn will be replaced by the fir tree, the wood of which is used for the making of frames for harps. The brier, known for its bitter, poisonous sting, is to be replaced by the glossy-leaved myrtle, with its white flowers and graceful perfume (Isa. 55:13).

This whole offer of guaranteed satisfaction is centered in the person of the Lord: "Seek ye the LORD while he may be found, call ye upon him while he is near" (Isa. 55:6). When the wicked forsakes his way and the unrighteous man his evil thoughts, and when they return to the Lord, then the Lord will have mercy and pardon their sins (Isa. 55:7). The Savior holds the key to satisfaction. If you want guaranteed satisfaction, accept Christ as your Savior and let Him be Lord of your life.

## GOOD NEWS FOR GOOD PEOPLE
### (Matt. 19:16-22)

Life must be frustrating for the good person who is not also a godly person. Jesus makes it possible for good people to also become godly people. It is one thing to have the plaudits of men but another thing to have the favorable pronouncement of God. A life, like a counterfeit bill, may appear to be quite similar to that which is valid but actually have no value when it comes to serving the purpose for which it was designed. The epitaph of the rich young ruler could well have been, "He went away sorrowful" (Matt. 19:22). It is too bad that he did not accept Christ's good news. He instead turned his back on Jesus. Watts, in his famous painting of the rich young ruler, so depicts him. A study comparing the Matthew account with Mark 10:17-22 and Luke 18:18-30 gives emphasis to the truths that follow.

*The rich young ruler was a person with promise.* He would have been envied by those who knew him. He was wealthy, young, highly principled, and prominent. He displayed excellent qualities of life. He was eager, humble, enthusiastic, courageous, discerning, sincere, and upright. He had all these favorable points, but still he was frustrated (Matt. 19:20).

*The rich young ruler was a person with a problem:* "What good thing shall I do, that I may have eternal life?" (Matt. 19: 16). He had kept the last six commandments, which pertain to one's relationships to his brethren, but he had overlooked the first four commandments, which concern one's relationship to God. To treat heaven and earth as though they were identical is foolish. Each has its own attributes, powers, and rewards. In terms of earthly things, man's sufficiency is always insufficient. If we stand on nothing but the earth, we stand as on a sinking ship. The rich young ruler had realized his lack of satisfaction but planned to get satisfaction on earth's terms. Lasting satisfaction just can never be found outside of the Savior (Isa. 55). Love for the world and the things in the world will crowd out love for God (1 John 2:15-17).

*The rich young ruler was a person with great possibilities.* He could have been a whole person, complete and mature (Matt. 19:21). He did not lack concern for the poor or charity. He lacked the lordship of Christ. Salvation is not something to be done but something to be received. Satisfaction is not possession, it is, rather, a condition. Satisfaction is not achievement but attitude. For the rich young ruler, becoming whole would have meant his giving up leadership and becoming a follower of Jesus Christ. Individuals with such great potential frequently find it extremely difficult to meet the qualifications for entering the kingdom of heaven (Matt. 19:24).

The rich young ruler was willing to bow the knee but not the will. He was willing to bow the head but not the heart. He was willing to yield obeisance but not obedience.

This individual knew what he needed, but he would not forgo what he wanted. He wanted heavenly treasures, but he was not willing to give up earthly trinkets. The Bible has good news for good people. They can become children of God (John 1:12). A person of promise who has a problem can discover unlimited possibilities when his life is yielded to the lordship of Christ. Unless Christ is Lord of all, He is not really Lord at all.

## What Will You Do with Jesus

> Pilate saith unto them, What shall I do then with Jesus which is called Christ? They all say unto him, Let him be crucified (Matt. 27:22).

Pilate had a problem. How could he get rid of Jesus? He faced the test of popularity, for the crowd said, "If thou let this man go, thou art not Caesar's friend" (John 19:12b). He faced the test of prestige, for his job was on the line. His wife urged him to have nothing to do with Jesus (Matt. 27:19). Five hearings were held regarding Jesus before nine o'clock in the morning. After all the trials, when Pilate saw that he was accomplishing nothing but that a riot was starting, He took water and washed his hands in front of the multitude, saying as he did so, "I am innocent of the blood of this just person: see ye to it" (Matt. 27:24).

Since A.D. 140, the people of God have learned and recited the Apostles' Creed and remembered that Pilate could not avoid the unavoidable Christ:

> I believe in God the Father Almighty; Maker of Heaven and earth; and in Jesus Christ His only Son our Lord; who was conceived by the Holy Ghost, born of the Virgin Mary; suffered under Pontius Pilate. . . .

184

We cannot avoid the unavoidable Christ. It is as though Christ were standing again in the judgment hall, friendless, forsaken, and betrayed by all. A call goes out again, What will you do with Jesus?

*It is impossible to avoid Christ through indifference.* They led Jesus from Caiaphas to the praetorium. Pilate sought to discover the charge that Jesus' accusers held against Him, but they avoided the issue. He finally told them to take and judge Jesus themselves. In John 18:38, Pilate said that he found no fault in Jesus. That did not satisfy the people in the mob. In John 19:6, they cried out for Him to be crucified. Pilate even sent Jesus to Herod for trial, but that did no good. Like the rich fool, Pilate wanted to leave God out of his thinking, planning, and philosophy of life; but he eventually had to deal with Him. Our relationship to Jesus cannot be settled by proxy.

*Pilate tried to avoid Jesus through mockery* (John 19:1-3). Have you ever stopped to meditate upon this scene? The Son of God wearing a crown of thorns; they put a reed in His hand, fell down in front of Him, and mocked Him (Matt. 27:29). They spat upon Him and beat Him. After scourging Jesus, they took Him away to be crucified. In John 18:37-38, Jesus had said that those who were of the truth would hear His voice. Pilate still had to deal with Him. We cannot avoid the unavoidable Christ through mockery.

Pilate made a third attempt to avoid having to deal with Jesus. *He tried to avoid Him through substitution* (John 18:39-40). But nothing and no one can take the place of Jesus.

W. E. Barton wrote a little book entitled *Four Unpublished Gospels.* He imagined in that book what the gospel account would say if Andrew, James, Judas, or John the Baptist had written the story of Jesus. I wish that someone would write the story of Jesus through the eyes of Barabbas. Try to capture in your mind his condition and his attitude. He had transgressed the law and was to die, but the cross that they had made for him was the one on which Jesus was crucified. Barabbas knew firsthand what it meant to have Jesus die in his place. Personality, kindness, culture, or even a human loved one cannot take the place of Jesus. There is no qualified substitute. Only Jesus, God's Son who knew no sin, can bear the penalty for our sin. There can be no substitute for Him.

It is as though Jesus were standing again in the judgment hall. As one hymnist put it, "Hearken! what meaneth the sudden call! What will you do with Jesus?"

### CHRIST MAKES THE DIFFERENCE
### (Mark 5:1-20)

Some people have suggested that it would be wise to begin one's Bible study with the gospel of Mark. It portrays Jesus at work. It is loaded with action, not words. In the sixteen chapters there are eighteen specific miracles and ten general references to miraculous work. The tone of action and straightforwardness is caught in the first two chapters with the frequent repetition of "straightway."

The incident recorded in Mark 5:1-20 is also referred to in two other gospels (Matt. 8:28-34; Luke 8:26-39). Little added touches are given to the account in each passage.

We cannot be certain of where the incident took place. We do know, however, that Jesus went there for a rest. That did not preclude His willingness at all times to help those in need. As the Master stepped onto the shore, a man with an unclean spirit rushed down the slope out of the tombs, and the man and the Master met (Mark 5:1-3). This contact with the Master brought about a shocking transformation. Meeting the Master meant a miracle. Change and challenge came to the evil spirits and to the sense of values and personal activity of the demoniac.

186

*Contact with Christ brought about a change from rebellion to reverence* (Mark 5:3-7). The man had been under bondage to evil. He was in isolation, dwelling in the tombs (Mark 5:3a). He was out of control (Mark 5:3-4). He had even gone to the point of self-mutilation (Mark 5:5). Satan had captivated his mind. Satan always desires to keep the mind in trash and trivia. The undisciplined mind is open to Satan's attack. It is important that we be aware of the designs of Satan lest he gain advantage over us (2 Cor. 2:11). When Jesus appeared on the scene, however, this rebellion was changed to reverence (Mark 5:6). Satan and the demons believe that God is one and shudder at the fact (James 2:19). They recognize that He and they cannot abide together. The incoming of Jesus means the outgoing of Satan.

*Contact with Christ brought about a change in values* (Mark 5:7b-13). Jesus commanded the evil spirits to come out of the tormented man. He allowed them to enter a herd of swine on the hillside, and two thousand swine ran violently down the hillside and into the sea to their deaths (Mark 5:10-13). At that point, the ones who cared for the swine asked Jesus to leave their country, because they had suffered the loss of their pigs, and that meant more to them than the freedom that had come to one individual (Mark 5:14-17). But when Jesus comes, people have preference over pigs. He has placed such a high value on the individual that no cost is too great to free even one from bondage. This truth is most clearly seen in God's gift of His Son (John 3:16).

*Contact with Christ brought about a change in activity* (Mark 5:18-20). The freed demoniac now sought the companionship of Christ (Mark 5:18). It may seem strange at first that Christ refused his request (Mark 5:19). But Jesus realized the power in a personal witness. He knew that the people in that locality would listen to one of their own. The man's most effective place of service was his own locality, where people could see with their eyes as well as hear with

187

their ears the evident freedom that had come through the
entering of Christ into his life.

The coming of Christ into a life still makes the difference.
He still can set the prisoner free; His grace availed for me.

### The Forsaken Waterpot
#### (John 4:1-42)

We learn much about people by listening to their conversations. You will find it profitable to locate, read, and study
the conversations between Jesus and various individuals in
the gospels. Several are located in the early chapters of John.
Some of the best-known are those wth Nicodemus (John 3),
the Samaritan woman (John 4), and the nobleman (John 4).
Jesus was interested in individuals and was never too busy to
converse with them.

Jesus left Judea in the south and went toward Galilee in
the north. It is recorded that He had to pass through Samaria
to do that (John 4:4). Such a route was not geographically
necessary, although Samaria was located between Judea and
Galilee. There were other roads He could have taken. It is
all the more unique that He went that way since the Jews
normally had no dealings with the Samaritans (John 4:9).

It was about noon when He came to a Samaritan city called
Sychar. Being weary (John 4:6), He sat down by a well to
rest. Soon a lady of Samaria came to draw water from the
well, and Jesus asked her for a drink of water. At that point
began a conversation that ended in a transformation. In the
conversation, Jesus asked a favor (John 4:7), aroused her
curiosity (John 4:10), taunted her sense of comfort (John
4:14), and induced her to seek something better (John 4:15).
In the course of the conversation He attracted the heart (John
4:4-9), arrested the mind (John 4:10-15), aroused the conscience (John 4:16-24), and assured the soul (John 4:25-30).
Jesus became very real to that lady as the conversation pro-
gressed. At first He was a Jew (John 4:9), then One who was

greater than Jacob (John 4:12), then a prophet (John 4:19), and finally the Messiah (John 4:29). As a result of that conversation, old ideas were changed, old prejudices were abandoned, and old ambitions were put aside. The waterpot that had marked the woman as a housewife was now laid aside, and she became a home missionary to invite the city to come out to meet Jesus.

*The conversation had revealed to her a source of possible satisfaction* (John 4:14). Jesus was positive in His approach, saying that He knew where there was a spring that would provide such satisfaction that she would never thirst again. It is tragic never to be thirsty. This is true both physically and spiritually. Blessed are the thirsty (Matt. 5:6). If they come to Christ, He will provide satisfaction (Isa. 55:1; Rev. 22:17). If you crave peace from distraction, purity from pollution, progress in grace, power in prayer, or pardon from sin, you can find satisfaction in Christ.

*The conversation had shown her the reality of her personal sin* (John 4:16-19). *Sin* is possibly the saddest word in the Bible. It separates and wounds. The woman immediately sought to change the subject of discussion by trying to involve Jesus in evaluating places of worship. He refused to be led to a discussion of places of worship when the crucial issue was the person who is to receive the worship. We have all sinned (Isa. 53:6). When a life has been soiled, it is greatly reduced in value.

*The conversation had revealed to the woman that she was facing a present Savior* (John 4:26). She had been waiting for the light and clinging to the promise, although the life was soiled. Jesus said, Your Deliverer is here right now. "Behold, now is the day of salvation" (2 Cor. 6:2).

When these three great revelations dawned upon her soul, the Samaritan woman could no longer be content to be just a housewife. She could no longer contain the good news. She had to tell the truth of Christ to others (John 4:29). She left her waterpot by the well and went to witness in the city. She started as a housewife, but after having a conversation with Christ, she became a home missionary.

## If You Are Thirsty

> If any man thirst, let him come unto me, and drink. He that believeth on me, as the scripture hath said, out of his belly shall flow rivers of living water (John 7:37-38).

David Wynbeek wrote a book entitled *The Beloved Yankee.* When I first saw the title I was intrigued, for I thought that it must be about a baseball player. To my surprise, it told the life story of a young man who lived only thirty years. His name was David Brainerd.

John Wesley, the founder of Methodism, asked his English church conference what could be done to help raise the low spiritual conditions of England. He then answered his own question by suggesting that each preacher read the life of David Brainerd and become followers of Brainerd, even as he had been a follower of Christ.

There were many contrasts between the mature Wesley and the young Brainerd. Wesley had been raised in a large family and lived to be almost ninety years old. Brainerd was raised in a Puritan home in Connecticut and was orphaned when only fourteen years old. At twenty-one, he said that he felt like a man reeling at the edge of the precipice of sin. By age thirty, he had fulfilled God's mission for his life, and God called him from his labors. His missionary labors with the American Indians had made a new chapter in Christian missions and had provided an enduring source of inspiration for Christian workers.

One portion of Scripture, John 7:37-52, characterizes Brainerd's life and work more than any other. The setting for that passage was Jerusalem during the Feast of Tabernacles. On the occasion of the Feast of Tabernacles, the priest would go every day to the Pool of Siloam with a golden pitcher, fill the pitcher with water, and then return with his people to the house of worship. On the last day of the feast, the eighth, the priest would go to the pool as he had done on the preceding seven days. But on that day he would not return with water. The golden pitcher would be empty. There was no water to pour into the silver vessel with holes in it that was located in the Temple. On that day there was no libation. The priest walked along the way with the empty pitcher as he returned to the Temple. As the procession headed by the priest came by in John 7:37, Jesus stood and cried with a loud voice, "If any man thirst, let him come unto me, and drink."

This cry of the Christ brought applause from some, division among others, hostility from others, and faith to still others. As David Brainerd preached on this text time and again and as others have before and after him, the same varied reactions have appeared.

The verse begins with a *condition*, "If any man thirst." Just as it would be tragic never to be thirsty physically, so it is also tragic never to have a real spiritual thirst. Spiritual thirst may be for peace in distraction, pardon for sin, progress in grace, purity from pollution, or power in prayer. The *invitation* "Let him come unto me, and drink" includes one of God's favorite words, *come*. We can come to Christ for safety, serenity, and satisfaction. The *prescription* is simple: "Drink." Faith has three constituents: longing for satisfaction, turning to the Savior, and finally receiving what He offers. The culmination presents a promised gratification: "He that believeth on me . . . out of his belly shall flow rivers of living water." We cannot help to satisfy the needs of others until there is an overflow from our own hearts.

> I came to Jesus, and I drank of that life-giving stream;
> My thirst was quenched, my soul revived, and now I live in Him.

HORATIUS BONAR

## A Song Before the Dawn
### (Acts 16:6-40)

God sometimes shifts the directions of our lives. Adoniram Judson tried to go to India but settled in Burma. David Livingstone tried to go to China but went instead to Africa. Paul tried to stay in Asia. He was forbidden to speak the Word in Asia (Acts 16:6), and after hearing the Macedonian call for help (Acts 16:9), he went to Europe. Fairbairn has said that Paul's gazing and going to Europe was the greatest event in history. God's providence is sometimes evidenced in His prohibitions. He sometimes gives the green light and sometimes the red. Paul was thus driven by divine preventives to the northwest extremity of Asia Minor.

This European invasion of the gospel started by a river at the place of prayer. Lydia, seller of purple, was the first European convert. God opened her heart, and she opened her home (Acts 16:13-15).

Then came the deliverance of the damsel who had the spirit of Pythoness. She was a demoniac, being subject to the powers of the evil spirit. There were those who made money from her ravings of insanity (Acts 16:16). When they realized that she had been delivered from the evil spirit and that their means of revenue had vanished, a riot resulted. Paul and Silas were considered the culprits and were thrown into prison (Acts 16:19-24). This was the price they had to pay for being willing to be involved.

Do not put a period there, however, for in man's extremity we see God's opportunity. God has power not only to change places but also people.

*The power of God changed Paul and Silas* (Acts 16:25-28). It would have been natural for them to complain. They were suffering for having done good. It was supernatural for them to worship. Within the prison cell at midnight, Paul and

Silas were praying and singing hymns. These were not prayers of petition but of adoration. While they worshiped, the other prisoners listened intently. God had given them power to sing in the midst of adverse circumstances. When the earthquake came, they paid no attention to it. Their primary concern was not the changing of circumstances so that they might escape but rather maintaining fellowship with God, who could provide songs in the night. They knew that problems are not solved by running from them.

Madam Guyon spent ten years in French prisons, from 1695 to 1705. During her confinement she wrote and sang song after song. A part of one of them went like this:

Nought have I else to do; I sing the whole day long,
And He whom most I love to please, doth listen to my
     song.
He caught and bound my wandering wing,
But still He bends to hear me sing.

*The power of God changed the prison keeper* (Acts 16:29-34). He had been sleeping while Paul and Silas had been singing. He had done his work, and nothing else mattered beyond sleep. Then came the panic. The earthquake had opened the prison doors. If the inmates had escaped, he had failed at his job. If that was the case, there was nothing left but suicide.

When word came that the prisoners were still there, the prison keeper had one question: "Sirs, what must I do to be saved?" (Acts 16:30). Paul and Silas then gave the spiritual answer to what he wondered in a physical sense. After Paul and Silas had provided instruction, the jailer washed their wounds (Acts 16:32-33). Having believed, he and his household were then baptized.

The song of Paul and Silas in the midst of adverse circumstances was used as a factor in bringing the dawn of salvation to the frustrated jailer.

## SALVATION, THEN SERVICE
### (1 Timothy 1:12-17)

Until we have received salvation in Christ, we cannot proclaim it. When we have received it, we cannot help but proclaim it. It is imperative that we clarify our own spiritual status before we contemplate serving the Savior as a communicator of the good news of salvation.

In 1 Timothy 1:12-17, Paul desired to strengthen timid Timothy for the spiritual battles that were ahead. Paul, then sixty-five years old, used his own salvation experience as an example for the thirty-five-year-old Timothy of the truth that the convicting, conquering power and love of Christ can subdue the greatest of foes.

We, like Paul, will do well to reflect upon our pasts. As we face the One altogether lovely, the Fairest of Ten Thousand, our own sense of unworthiness is magnified. Paul recalled that he had abused, persecuted, and insulted Christ (1 Tim. 1:13). He had been, in fact, an insolent man, or as Way said in his translation, "a brutal ruffian." It was of this same Paul that Ananias said, "I have heard by many of this man, how much evil he hath done to thy saints" (Acts 9:13). You and I, like Paul, were sinners.

Then to us in our misery came mercy. Paul said, "But I obtained mercy, because I did it ignorantly in unbelief" (1 Tim. 1:13b). I am afraid that some of us were in a worse state than Paul, since we knew better but did not do better. In spite of our sinfulness, the grace of God flowed superabundantly with faith and love that are centered in Christ Jesus (1 Tim. 1:14). Through His abounding grace, He not only saved us but also counted us faithful, appointing us to His service. Salvation leads to service. Let us not speak in general terms, but let us say with Paul, "I thank him that enabled me, even Christ Jesus our Lord, for that he counted me faithful, appointing me to his service" (1 Tim. 1:12, ASV).

We, like Paul, will do well to reach toward the future so that we can clarify in our thinking the purpose for such great mercy. "Yet, mercy was shown me for the very purpose that in my case as the foremost of sinners Jesus might display His perfect patience, to make me an example to those who in the future might believe on Him to obtain eternal life" (1 Tim. 1:16, Williams): this statement occurs five times in the pastoral epistles and no where else in the New Testament. The true story includes mystery in that "Christ Jesus came into the world," and adventure in that He came "to save sinners" (1 Tim. 1:15). We have this same message of mercy to share with a lost world. It is the supreme love story.

Nothing can stop the geyser of praise that erupts from the heart that has known the marvelous mercy of God. There comes out of the soul of the apostle, inspired by the Spirit of God, a phrase used only here by Paul: "Now unto the King eternal" (1 Tim. 1:17). He is the immortal (Rom. 1:23), invisible (Col. 1:15), and only God (1 Tim. 1:17). To the God of all mercies "be honour and glory for ever and ever (1 Tim. 1:17).

Until we have received salvation, we cannot proclaim it. When we have received it, we cannot help but proclaim it.


## QUESTIONS AT THE BORDER
### (1 John 3:1-24)

One writer has suggested that the gospel of John leads us across the threshold of the Father's house and that 1 John makes us at home there. The certainty of having crossed the threshold is confirmed by 1 John 5:13: "These things have I written unto you that believe on the name of the Son of God; that ye may know that ye have eternal life, and that ye may believe on the name of the Son of God." As one becomes a child of God, he passes from the land of death into the land of life. He receives citizenship papers in the colony of heaven (Phil. 3:20).

What questions are posed to an individual as he passes from one country to another? There are normally three, and those three questions at the border unlock the content of 1 John 3. *First, Where were you born?* "*Now are we children of God*" (1 John 3:2a, ASV). Just think of the love that made it possible for us to be called the children of God (1 John 3:1). We were born first as children of men, but then we were born again, and through this spiritual birth we became children of God (Gal. 3:26). This new birth was necessary (John 3:3). Our nature demanded it, our search for forgiveness demanded it, and God commanded it. The nature of the new birth defies human explanation. But just as we can feel the wind and know that it blows even though we cannot see it, so everyone who is born of the spirit of God eventually senses the transformation and knows that it is real (John 3:7-8). This new-birth experience is as near as a believing "look" (John 3:14-15). Amazing love has made all of this possible. Christian living involves discipleship, stewardship, worship, lordship, fellowship, and an inheritance, but it all begins with sonship.

*Second, What are you taking with you?* There are three items. The first is victory over sin (1 John 3:4-10): "No one who lives in him keeps on sinning" (1 John 3:6, NIV). To sin is unlawful (1 John 3:4), illogical (1 John 3:5), and unspiritual (1 John 3:8). The next item we are taking with us is love for one another (1 John 3:11-18). Love is a sign that we have passed from death to life (1 John 3:14). This love demands sacrifice (1 John 3:16). The third item we are taking with us is confidence toward God (1 John 3:19-24). Check the notes of certainty in verses 19, 20, and 24. "If our heart condemn us not, then have we confidence toward God" (1 John 3:21).

*Finally, Where are you going?* "*Now are we the sons of God, and it doth not yet appear what we shall be: but we know that, when he shall appear, we shall be like him; for we shall see him as he is*" (1 John 3:2). We are going to be with God. As the root turns to the rose, the caterpillar to the butterfly, and the acorn to the oak, so in a moment shall we all be changed, although we do not know yet just what it will be like. (1 Cor. 15:51-52). Jesus Christ is going to come again (Acts 1:11), and then we shall see Him and be like Him. He is coming back for His children (John 14:1-3). We are not like the thirty-two million letters in the dead-letter office that are not going anywhere because their destination is indefinite. Our destination is clear. We are going to be with Christ, the One who died for our sins and rose from the tomb for our justification.

Make certain that you have the correct answers for the three questions asked at the border.

Where were you born?
What are you taking with you?
Where are you going?

# Bibliography

Aᴍᴇʀɪᴄᴀɴ Wᴏʀᴋs ɪɴ Hᴏᴍɪʟᴇᴛɪᴄ Tʜᴇᴏʀʏ Hᴀᴠɪɴɢ Rᴇʟᴇᴠᴀɴᴄᴇ
ᴛᴏ Eᴠᴀɴɢᴇʟɪsᴛɪᴄ Pʀᴇᴀᴄʜɪɴɢ

Pʀɪᴍᴀʀʏ sᴏᴜʀᴄᴇs

Abbey, Merrill R. *Living Doctrine in a Vital Pulpit.* Nashville: Abingdon, 1964.

Baumann, J. Daniel. *An Introduction to Contemporary Preaching.* Grand Rapids: Baker, 1972.

Blackwood, Andrew W. *Expository Preaching for Today.* Nashville: Abingdon-Cokesbury, 1953.

———. *Biographical Preaching for Today.* Nashville: Abingdon, 1954.

———. *Doctrinal Preaching for Today.* Nashville: Abingdon, 1956.

Brastow, Lewis O. *The Work of the Preacher: A Study of Homiletical Principles and Methods.* New York: Pilgrim, 1914.

Breed, David R. *Preparing to Preach.* New York: Doran, 1911.

Broadus, John A. *On the Preparation and Delivery of Sermons.* Rev. ed. Edited by Jesse B. Weatherspoon. New York: Harper & Bros., 1944.

Brown, H. C., Jr. *A Quest for Reformation in Preaching.* Waco, Tex.: Word, 1968.

Brown, H. C., Jr.; Clinard, H. Gordon; and Northcutt, Jesse J. *Steps to the Sermon.* Nashville: Broadman, 1963.

Burrell, David J. *The Sermon: Its Construction and Delivery.* New York: Revell, 1913.

Caemmerer, Richard R. *Preaching for the Church.* St. Louis: Concordia, 1959.

Clowney, Edmund P. *Preaching and Biblical Theology.* Grand Rapids: Eerdmans, 1961.

Coffin, Henry Sloane. *What to Preach.* New York: Doran, 1926.

Davis, Ozora S. *Evangelistic Preaching*. New York: Revell, 1921.
———. *Using the Bible in Public Address*. New York: Association Press, 1916.
Etter, John W. *The Preacher and His Sermon*. Dayton, Ohio: Breth., 1891.
Hiltner, Seward. *Ferment in the Ministry*. Nashville: Abingdon, 1969.
Hoyt, Arthur S. *The Pulpit and American Life*. New York: Macmillan, 1921.
Johnson, Herrick. *The Ideal Ministry*. New York: Revell, 1908.
Jordan, G. Ray. *You Can Preach*. New York: Revell, 1951.
———. *Preaching During a Revolution*. Anderson, Ind.: Warner, 1962.
Koller, Charles W. *Expository Preaching Without Notes*. Grand Rapids: Baker, 1962.
Leavell, Roland. *Prophetic Preaching Then and Now*. Grand Rapids: Baker, 1963.
Pearce, J. Winston. *Planning Your Preaching*. Nashville: Broadman, 1967.
Perry, Lloyd M. *Biblical Sermon Guide*. Grand Rapids: Baker, 1970.
———. *Biblical Preaching for Today's World*. Chicago: Moody, 1973.
Riley, W. B. *The Preacher and His Preaching*. Wheaton, Ill.: Sword of the Lord, 1948.
Short, Roy H. *Evangelistic Preaching*. Nashville: Tidings, 1946.
Skinner, Craig. *The Teaching Ministry of the Pulpit*. Grand Rapids: Baker, 1973.
Stanfield, V. L. *Effective Evangelistic Preaching*. Grand Rapids: Baker, 1965.
Weatherspoon, Jesse B. *Sent Forth to Preach*. New York: Harper & Bros., 1954.
Whitesell, Faris D. *Evangelistic Preaching and the Old Testament*. Chicago: Moody, 1947.

SECONDARY SOURCES

Baxter, Batsell. *The Heart of the Yale Lectures*. New York: Macmillan, 1947.

Beecher, Henry Ward. *The Yale Lectures on Preaching*. 2d series. New York: Ford, 1873.

Blackwood, Andrew W. *The Preparation of Sermons*. Nashville: Abingdon-Cokesbury, 1948.

———. "Evangelism and Preaching." *Contemporary Evangelical Thought*. Edited by Carl F. H. Henry. New York: Channel, 1957.

Bowie, Walter R. *Preaching*. Nashville: Abingdon, 1954.

Cadman, S. Parker. *Ambassadors of God*. New York: Macmillan, 1920.

Coffin, Henry Sloane. *In a Day of Social Rebuilding*. New Haven: Yale U., 1918.

Davis, Grady. *Design for Preaching*. Philadelphia: Muhlenberg, 1958.

Fuller, Davis Otis, ed. *Spurgeon's Lectures to His Students*. 2d ed. Grand Rapids: Zondervan, 1945.

Graves, Henry C. *Lectures on Homiletics*. Philadelphia: Am. Bapt. Pub. Soc., 1906.

Hoppin, James. *Homiletics*. New York: Dodd, Mead, 1881.

Hoyt, Arthur S. *The Preacher: His Person, Message and Method*. New York: Macmillan, 1909.

Jones, Bob, Jr. *How to Improve Your Preaching*. New York: Revell, 1945.

Kern, John A. *The Ministry to the Congregation*. New York: Jennings & Graham, 1897.

———. *Vision and Power*. New York: Revell, 1915.

Lee, Mark W. *The Minister and His Ministry*. Grand Rapids: Zondervan, 1960.

McCracken, Robert J. *The Making of the Sermon*. New York: Harper & Bros., 1956.

Moore, W. T. *Preacher Problems or the Twentieth-Century Preacher at His Work*. New York: Revell, 1907.

Nichole, Thomas M. *Preaching*. Philadelphia: Presby. Bd. of Pub., 1904.

Phelps, Austin. *The Theory of Preaching*. New York: Scribner's, 1894.

Pittenger, W. Norman. *Proclaiming Christ Today*. Greenwich, Conn.: Seabury, 1962.

Sanford, Jack O. *Make Your Preaching Relevant*. Nashville: Broadman, 1963.

Schloerb, Rolland W. *The Preaching Ministry Today*. New York: Harper & Bros., 1946.

Schroeder, Frederick W. *Preaching the Word with Authority*. Philadelphia: Westminster, 1954.

Shedd, W. G. T. *Treatise on Homiletics and Pastoral Theology*. New York: Scribner's, 1867.

Sleeth, Ronald E. *Proclaiming the Word*. Nashville: Abingdon, 1964.

Sweazey, George E. *Preaching the Good News*. Englewood Cliffs, N.J.: Prentice-Hall, 1976.

Whitesell, Faris D. *The Art of Biblical Preaching*. Grand Rapids: Zondervan, 1950.

Worley, Robert C. *Preaching and Teaching in the Earliest Church*. Philadelphia: Westminster, 1967.

## Non-American Works in Homiletic Theory Having Relevance to Evangelistic Preaching

### Secondary Sources

Allan, Arthur. *The Art of Preaching*. London: Clarke, 1939.

Cowan, Arthur A. *The Primacy of Preaching Today*. New York: Scribner's, 1955.

Dale, R. W. *Nine Lectures on Preaching*. Chicago: Barnes, 1877.

Dodd, C. H. *The Apostolic Preaching and Its Developments*. New York: Harper & Bros., 1936.

Garvie, Alford E. *The Christian Preacher*. Edinburgh: T. & T. Clark, 1920.

———. *A Guide to Preachers*. London: Hodder & Stoughton, 1911.

Horne, Charles S. *The Romance of Preaching*. New York: Revell, 1914.

Jarvis E. D. *If Any Man Minister*. London: Hodder & Stoughton, 1951.

Lehman, H. T. *Heralds of the Gospel*. Philadelphia: Muhlenberg, 1953.

Lloyd-Jones, D. Martyn. *Preaching and Preachers*. Grand Rapids: Zondervan, 1972.

McComb, Samuel. *Preaching in Theory and Practice*. New York: Oxford U., 1926.

Menzies, Robert. *Preaching and Pastoral Evangelism*. Edinburgh: St. Andrews, n.d.

Niles, Daniel T. *The Preacher's Calling to Be Servant*. New York: Harper & Bros., 1959.

Reid, James. *In Quest of Reality*. New York: Doran, n.d.

Sangster, W. E. *The Craft of Sermon Construction*. London: Epworth, 1951.

Soper, Donald. *The Advocacy of the Gospel*. Nashville: Abingdon, 1961.

Stewart, James. *Heralds of God*. London: Hodder & Stoughton, 1946.

Waterhouse, Eric S. *Psychology and Pastoral Work*. Nashville: Cokesbury, 1940.

## AMERICAN WORKS OF EVANGELISTIC THEORY HAVING RELEVANCE TO EVANGELISTIC PREACHING

PRIMARY SOURCES

Autry, C. E. *Basic Evangelism*. Grand Rapids: Zondervan, 1959.

Ayer, William W. *Flame for the Altar*. Grand Rapids: Zondervan, 1952.

Biederwolf, William E. *Evangelism: Its Justification, Its Operation and Its Value*. New York: Revell, 1921.

Blackwood, Andrew W. *Evangelism in the Home Church*. Nashville: Abingdon-Cokesbury, 1942.

Chapman, J. Wilbur. *The Problem of the Work*. New York: Doran, 1911.

Crossland, Weldon. *How to Increase Church Membership and Attendance*. Nashville: Abingdon-Cokesbury, 1949.

Doe, Walter P., ed. *Eminent Authors on Effective Revival Preaching*. Providence, R.I.: Greene, 1876.

Finney, Charles G. *Lectures on Revivals of Religion*. New York: Leavitt, Lord, 1835.

Ford, Leighton. *The Christian Persuader*. New York: Harper & Row, 1966.

Goodell, Charles L. "Preaching the Evangel." *Catching Men.* Edited by J. P. Brushingham. Cincinnati: Jennings & Graham, 1906.

————. *Pastoral and Personal Evangelism.* New York: Revell, 1907.

Grindstaff, W. E. *Ways to Win.* Nashville: Broadman, 1957.

Hervey, G. W. *Manual of Revivals.* New York: Funk & Wagnalls, 1884.

Kerr, Phil. *Music In Evangelism.* Grand Rapids: Zondervan, 1962.

Mott, John R., ed. *Evangelism for the World Today.* New York: Harper & Bros., 1938.

Muncy, W. L. *New Testament Evangelism for Today.* Kansas City: Central Sem., 1941.

North, Harry M. *Harvest and Reapers.* Nashville: Cokesbury, 1931.

Packer, J. I. *Evangelism and the Sovereignty of God.* Downers Grove, Ill.: InterVarsity, 1961.

Porter, James. *Revivals of Religion.* Boston: Pierce, 1849.

Roberts, B. T. *Fishers of Men.* Rochester, N.Y.: Roberts, 1892.

Scarborough, L. R. *With Christ After the Lost.* New York: Doran, 1919.

Stone, John T. *Winning Men.* New York: Revell, 1946.

Sumner, Robert L. *Evangelism: The Church On Fire.* Chicago: Reg. Bapt., 1960.

Sweazey, George E. *Effective Evangelism: The Greatest Work in the World.* New York: Harper & Bros., 1953.

Taylor, Frederick E. *The Evangelistic Church.* Philadelphia: Judson, 1927.

Templeton, Charles B. *Evangelism for Tomorrow.* New York: Harper & Bros., 1957.

Torrey, Reuben A. *How to Work for Christ.* New York: Revell, 1901.

Whitesell, Faris D. *Basic New Testament Evangelism.* Grand Rapids: Zondervan, 1949.

————. *Sixty-Five Ways to Give Evangelistic Invitations.* Grand Rapids: Zondervan, 1945.

Wilson, John. *An Introduction to Church Music*. Chicago: Moody, 1965.

Work, Edgar W. *Every Minister His Own Evangelist*. New York: Revell, 1927.

SECONDARY SOURCES

Anderson, George W. "Evangelism and the Public Revival." *Are You An Evangelist?* Edited by Edwin H. Hughes. Nashville: Abingdon-Cokesbury, 1936.

Bader, Jesse M. *Evangelism in a Changing America*. St. Louis: Bethany, 1957.

Chapman, J. Wilbur. *Present-Day Evangelism*. New York: Baker & Taylor, 1903.

Daniels, E. J. *Techniques of Torchbearing*. Grand Rapids: Zondervan, 1957.

Dobbins, Gaines S. *Evangelism According to Christ*. New York: Harper & Bros., 1949.

Fish, Henry C. *Handbook of Revivals*. Boston: Earle, 1874.

Fosdick, Harry E. "What's the Matter with Preaching?" *Re-Thinking Evangelism*. Edited by George G. Hunter. Nashville: Tidings, 1971.

Gilbert, Levi. *Dynamic Christianity*. New York: Eaton & Mains, 1912.

Goodard, O. E. *Modern Evangelism on Fundamental Lines*. Nashville: Cokesbury, 1924.

Goodell, Charles L. *The Pastor His Own Evangelist*. Cleveland: Barton, 1911.

———. *Motives and Methods in Modern Evangelism*. New York: Revell, 1926.

Green, O. Olin. *Normal Evangelism*. New York: Revell, 1910.

Hale, Joe. *Design for Evangelism*. Nashville: Tidings, 1969.

Hallock, G. B. F. *The Evangelistic Cyclopedia*. New York: Smith, 1930.

Hannan, F. Watson. *Evangelism*. New York: Meth. Book Concern, 1921.

Homrighausen, Elmer G. *Choose Ye This Day*. Philadelphia: Westminster, 1943.

Joseph, Oscar L. *Essentials of Evangelism.* New York: Doran, 1918.

Leavell, Roland. *Evangelism: Christ's Imperative Commission.* Nashville: Broadman, 1951.

Leonard, A. W. *Evangelism in the Remaking of the World.* New York: Meth. Book Concern, 1919.

Lowry, Oscar. *Scripture Memory for Successful Soul-winning.* Grand Rapids: Zondervan, 1932.

Massee, J. C. *Evangelism in the Local Church.* Philadelphia: Judson, 1939.

Morgan, G. Campbell. *Evangelism.* New York: Revell, 1904.

Mosley, J. Edward, ed. *Evangelism: Commitment and Involvement.* St. Louis: Bethany, 1965.

Newall, William W. *Revivals How and When?* New York: Armstrong & Son, 1882.

Peck, Jonas O. *The Revival and the Pastor.* New York: Eaton & Mains, 1894.

Rees, Paul S. *Stir Up the Gift.* Grand Rapids: Zondervan, 1952.

Rice, Merton S. "Evangelism and the Pulpit." *Are You An Evangelist?* Edited by Edwin H. Hughes. Nashville: Abingdon-Cokesbury, 1936.

Rockey, Carroll C. *Scriptural Evangelism.* Philadelphia: U. Luth., 1925.

Rust, Charles H. *Practical Ideals in Evangelism.* Philadelphia: Griffith & Rowland, 1906.

Sellers, James E. *The Outsider and the Word of God.* Nashville: Abingdon, 1961.

Short, Roy H. *Evangelism through the Local Church.* Nashville: Abingdon, 1956.

Stewart, Wentworth F. *The Evangelistic Awakening.* Cincinnati: Jennings & Graham, 1905.

Thomson, D. P., ed. *The Modern Evangelistic Address.* New York: Doran, 1925.

Torrey, R. A. *How to Promote and Conduct a Successful Revival.* New York: Revell, 1901.

Wagner, James E. *Rural Evangelism.* New York: Meth. Book Concern, 1920.

Webb, Aquilla. *One Thousand Evangelistic Illustrations.* New York: Doran, 1921.

Weber, H. C. *Evangelism: A Graphic Survey.* New York: Macmillan, 1929.

## NON-AMERICAN WORKS OF EVANGELISTIC THEORY HAVING RELEVANCE TO EVANGELISTIC PREACHING

### SECONDARY SOURCES

Barclay, William. *Fishers of Men.* Philadelphia: Westminster, 1966.

Broomhall, A. J. *Time for Action.* Chicago: Inter-Varsity, 1965.

Dawson, William J. *The Evangelistic Note.* New York: Revell, 1905.

Fletcher, Lionel B. *The Effective Evangelist.* New York: Doran, 1923.

Green, Bryan, *The Practice of Evangelism.* New York: Scribner's, 1951.

Neil, Samuel G. *A Great Evangelism.* Philadelphia: Judson, 1929.

Pierson, Arthur T. *Evangelistic Work in Principle and Practice.* London: Dickenson, 1888.

Spurgeon, Charles H. *The Soul-Winner.* Condensed and edited by David O. Fuller. Grand Rapids: Zondervan, 1948.

Walker, Alan. *The Whole Gospel for the Whole World.* Nashville: Abingdon, 1957.

Webster, Douglas. *What is Evangelism?* London: Salisbury Square, 1959.

White, F. C. *Evangelism Today.* London: Marshall, Morgan & Scott, n.d.

## HISTORY OF PREACHING

### PRIMARY SOURCES

Broadus, John A. *Lectures on the History of Preaching.* New York: Armstrong & Son, 1902.

Dargan, Edwin C. *A History of Preaching.* 2 vols. Grand Rapids: Baker, 1954.

McLoughlin, William G. J. *Modern Revivalism: Charles G. Finney to Billy Graham.* New York: Ronald, 1959.

Pattison, T. H. *The History of Christian Preaching*. Philadelphia: Am. Bapt. Pub. Soc., 1903.

Webber, F. R. *A History of Preaching in Britain and America*. 3 vols. Milwaukee: Northwestern, 1952-57.

SECONDARY SOURCES

Abbott, Lyman, et. al. *The Prophets of the Christian Faith*. New York: Macmillan, 1896.

Beardsley, F. G. *A History of American Revivals*. New York: Tract Soc., 1904.

———. *Religious Progress Through Revivals*. New York: Tract Soc., 1904.

Blackwood, A. W., ed. *The Protestant Pulpit*. Nashville: Abingdon-Cokesbury, 1947.

———. *Preaching in Time of Reconstruction*. New York: Pulpit, 1945.

Chrisman, Lewis H. *The Message of the American Pulpit*. New York: Smith, 1930.

Dargan, Edwin C. *The Art of Preaching in Light of Its History*. New York: Doran, 1922.

Fischer, Harold A. *Reviving Revivals*. Springfield, Mo.: Gospel Pub. House, 1950.

Hudson, Winthrop S. *The Great Tradition of the American Churches*. New York: Harper & Bros., 1953.

Kerr, Hugh T. *Preaching in the Early Church*. Westwood, N.J.: Revell, 1942.

Lacy, B. R. *Revivals in the Midst of the Years*. Richmond: Knox, 1943.

Muncy, W. L. *A History of Evangelism in the United States*. Kansas City: Central Sem., 1945.

Niebuhr, H. Richard, and Williams, Daniel D., eds. *The Ministry in Historical Perspective*. New York: Harper & Bros., 1956.

Strickland, Arthur B. *The Great American Revival*. Cincinnati: Standard, 1934.

Sweet, W. W. *Revivalism in America*. New York: Scribner's, 1944.

Thompson, Ernest T. *Changing Emphases in American Preaching*. Philadelphia: Westminster, 1943.

Wilkinson, William C. *Modern Masters of Pulpit Discourse.* New York: Funk & Wagnalls, 1905.

## THESES AND DISSERTATIONS

Abernathy, Elton. "An Analysis of Trends in American Homiletical Theory since 1860." Ph.D. dissertation, State University of Iowa, 1941.

Gulick, Joseph I. "A Survey of American Preaching." Master's thesis, George Washington University, 1933.

Hardy, Richard B. "Kerygmatic Preaching." Th.M. thesis, Union Theological Seminary in Virginia, 1958.

Higgins, Howard H. "A Critical Study of Selected Books on Preaching Published in the United States before 1861." Master's thesis, State University of Iowa, 1927.

Hjertman, Wendell E. "The Pastor As His Own Pulpit Evangelist." Th.M. thesis, Northern Baptist Theological Seminary, 1962.

Hunter, George G. "Evangelistic Rhetoric in Secular Britain: the Theory and Speaking of Donald Soper and Bryan Green." Ph.D. dissertation, Northwestern University, 1972.

Lacour, L. L. "A Study of the Revival Method in America 1920-1955, With Special Reference to Billy Sunday, Aimee Semple McPherson and Billy Graham." Ph.D. dissertation, Northwestern University, 1956.

Lambertson, Floyd W. "Survey and Analysis of American Homiletics Prior to 1860." Ph.D. dissertation, State University of Iowa, 1930.

Maeda, Eizho. "A Study of the Evangelistic Preaching of Selected American Evangelists in an Attempt to Discover Evangelistic Preaching Principles Which Would Be Effective in Japanese Evangelism." Th.M. thesis, Trinity Evangelical Divinity School, 1971.

Perry, Lloyd M. "Trends and Emphases in the Philosophy, Materials and Methodology of American Protestant Homiletic Education as Established by a Study of Selected Trade and Textbooks Published Between 1834 and 1954." Ph.D. dissertation, Northwestern University, 1961.

## Journal Articles

Brunsting, Bernard. "Evangelistic Preaching." *Christianity Today* 7 (1962) :120-22.

Caplan, Harry, and King, Henry H. "Pulpit Eloquence: A List of Doctoral and Historical Studies in English." *Speech Monographs* 22 (1955) :5-159.

Coleman, Robert E. "An Evangelistic Sermon Checklist." *Christianity Today* 10 (1965) :27-28.

"Epochal Event: What God Did in Korea." *Christianity Today* 17 (1973) :1009-10.

Graham, Billy. "Why the Berlin Congress?" *Christianity Today* 11 (1966) :131-35.

Kucharsky, David. "Will the Saints Go Marching Out?" *Christianity Today* 14 (1970) :1139-41.

———. "Getting It Together for Jesus." *Christianity Today* 16 (1972) :964-66.

"The Lausanne Covenant." *Christianity Today* 18 (1974) :1244-46.

Little, Paul E. "Looking Ahead to Lausanne." *Christianity Today* 17 (1973) :208-10.

Morris, Leon. "Australian Evangelicals: Up from Down Under." *Christianity Today* 16 (1971) :48-50.

Nogosek, Robert J. "For a Renewal of Preaching." *Worship* 38 (1964) :283-88.

Ramientos, Eustaquio, Jr. "Why an Asian-South Pacific Congress?" *Christianity Today* 12 (1968) :877-78.

Rawlings, Elden. "Bogata: Latin Liason." *Christianity Today* 14 (1969) :281.

"U. S. Congress on Evangelism: A Turning Point?" *Christianity Today* 14 (1969) :28-29.

Van Capelleveen, Jan J. "European Congress: 'Getting to Know You.'" *Christianity Today* 15 (1971) :1160-61.

Weatherspoon, Jesse B. "The Evangelistic Sermon." *Review and Expositor* 62 (1945) :59-67.

## Classical Rhetoric

Baldwin. *Medieval Rhetoric and Poetic.* Gloucester, Mass.: Smith, 1959.

Clark, Donald L. *Rhetoric in Greco-Roman Education.* New York: Columbia U., 1957.

Cooper, Lane. *The Rhetoric of Aristotle.* New York: Appleton-Century, 1932.

Crocker, Lionel. *Argumentation and Debate.* New York: Am. Book, 1944.

Mudd, Charles S., and Sillars, Malcolm O. *Speech Content and Communication.* San Francisco: Chandler, 1962.

Oliver, Robert T. *The Psychology of Persuasive Speech.* New York: Longmans, Green, 1942.

Perry, Lloyd M. "Sermon Style in Contemporary Terms." In *Baker's Dictionary of Practical Theology,* edited by Ralph G. Turnbull, pp. 74-81. Grand Rapids: Baker, 1967.

Thonssen, Lester, ed. *Selected Readings in Rhetoric and Public Speaking.* New York: Wilson, 1942.

Thonssen, Lester, and Baird, A. Craig. *Speech Criticism: The Development of Standards for Rhetorical Appraisal.* New York: Ronald, 1948.

Whately, Richard. *Elements of Rhetoric.* London: Parker, 1850.

Woolbert, Charles H., and Nelson, Severina. *The Art of Interpretive Speech.* New York: Crofts, 1935.

OTHER WORKS

Arthur, William. *The Tongue of Fire.* Winona Lake, Ind.: Light and Life, n.d.

Bounds, E. M. *Power Through Prayer.* London: Marshall, Morgan and Scott, n.d.

Dijk, Karl. *De Dienst der Prediking.* Kampen, Netherlands: Koh, 1955.

Hoekstra, Tjeerd. *Gereformeerde Homiletiek.* Wageningen: Zomer, n.d.

Jowett, J. H. *The Preacher: His Life and Work.* London: Hodder & Stoughton, n.d.

Ker, John. *Lectures on the History of Preaching.* Edited by A. R. Macewen. New York: Armstrong & Son, 1889.

Kuyper, Abraham. *Encyclopaedia der Heilige Godgeleerheid,* v. 3. Amsterdam, Netherlands: J. A. Wormser, 1894.

211

Lewis, Ralph L. *Speech for Persuasive Preaching.* Berne, Ind.: n.p., 1968.

McLaughlin, Raymond W. *Communication for the Church.* Grand Rapids: Zondervan, 1968.

Meyer, F. B. *Expository Preaching Plans and Methods.* Toronto: Upper Can. Tract Soc., 1910.

Mortenson, C. David, ed. *Basic Readings in Communication Theory.* New York: Harper & Row, 1973.

Spurgeon, Charles H. *Lectures to My Students.* London: Passmore and Alabaster, 1875.

Turnbull, Ralph G., ed. *Baker's Dictionary of Practical Theology.* Grand Rapids: Baker, 1967.

Vinet, A. *Pastoral Theology: Or the Theory of the Evangelical.* Edited and translated by Thomas H. Skinner. New York: Harper & Bros., 1853.

Whitney, Frederick L. *The Elements of Research.* 3d ed. Englewood Cliffs, N.J.: Prentice-Hall, 1950.

# Index of Persons

213

214

## DATE DUE

| DEC 17 '80 | | | |
|---|---|---|---|
| MAY 6 '81 | | | |
| SEP 15 '82 | | | |
| DEC 7 '83 | | | |
| F | | | |
| MAR 25 '87 | | | |
| APR 8 '87 | | | |
| | | | |
| | | | |
| | | | |
| | | | |
| | | | |
| | | | |
| | | | |
| | | | |
| | | | |
| | | | |